FROM DARKNESS TO LIGHT: A STORY OF A SOUL IN DARKNESS

By: Ruben s.

Order this book online at www.trafford.com
or email orders@trafford.com

Most Trafford titles are also available at major online book retailers.

Printed in the United States of America.

ISBN: 978-1-4269-4539-7 (sc)
ISBN: 978-1-4269-4615-8 (hc)
ISBN: 978-1-4269-4616-5 (e)

Library of Congress Control Number: 2010915292

*Our mission is to efficiently provide the world's finest, most comprehensive book publishing
service, enabling every author to experience success. To find out how to publish your book,
your way, and have it available worldwide, visit us online at www.trafford.com*

Trafford rev. 11/04/2010

 www.trafford.com

North America & international
toll-free: 1 888 232 4444 (USA & Canada)
phone: 250 383 6864 ♦ fax: 812 355 4082

Dedicated with all my love to the loving memory of my mother Gladys M Gonzalez to whom by no fault of her own this disease indirectly affected her choices and decisions to the point of dying a violent death. To the memory of my father Andino S Rios who became a victim to this sickness of the soul and the incredible malady of the mind and to the thousands who lose their lives daily because the level of darkness doesn't allow them to find hope. To my great friend and brother Ciro Jerry P, my thanks to you.

May The Lord Bless you All

Table of Contents

__Introduction__

From Darkness to Light is a true account of the author's life. Some of the names of the people mentioned herein have been changed with the purpose of granting them some mental peace during the daily course of their personal lives. It is my intention and my utmost desire to be able to bring to the reader a story with which he/she may be able to identify his/her pain and his/her failures. It is in no way my intention to attempt to change anyone's life, but instead through my story, I wish to bring to the reader a bit of hope so that he/she may see the reality of his/her life and where your current path will take you. I have not written this account to portray myself as a fearless, brave, intelligent, or grandiose person, as these characteristics don't exist when it comes to the personal destruction of a human being. It is of utmost importance that the reader be able to see and identify those areas that are creating problems in his/her life and without comparing them, be able to address correct and remove them. If any of those areas are affected by the use and abuse of alcohol, controlled substances, or problems within the nucleus of the family and the community, and it is my hope that this story will serve as a foundation for you to resume life and find freedom from the destructive force that is addiction in order for you to be able to once again become a productive member of society.

Forward by the Author

Throughout many years of personal destruction and suffering, God saw fit to rescue me from the worst enemy that exists   myself. It has been with acquired mental clarity that my destructive heart has today been able get out of such painful darkness which I caused to myself and countless others who were not responsible for the mental maladjustments and unhealthy suffering that I experienced. To be able to awake in the morning and to know in my mind that the obsession and compulsion for alcohol and controlled substances no longer exists within me is the most valuable gift that God has granted me, and not having to live chained in that dark and destructive prison has been the freedom that my spirit so greatly needed. It is with this thought in mind that for just these 24 hours, my gift of the day is enjoyed, and I know very well that I can't do anything about my past. I also keep in mind that tomorrow has not yet arrived, and it's because of this that I live today to the fullest, because just for today, I can work with this destructive sickness.

<u>Acknowledgements</u>

The greatest thanks for this story is given to my God, to the memory of my mother, Gladys Maria Gonzales, and to my father, Andino S. Rios, for by their birth they granted purpose to my life under God's creation. With this in mind, I wish to offer my sincerest thanks to Trafford Publishing and Mr. Demond D. Jefferson , Publishing Consultant at Trafford Publishing and also to all of their staff who have contributed to making this project possible. I also wish to thank all of the people who throughout the years have provided me with healthy examples and who have brought with their knowledge and love something incredible to my life. To my daughter, Ivette S. for understanding my shortcomings and remaining in my life despite them. To my son Ruben S Jr. for understanding the seriousness of this disease and for today being patient and focused with his life and achieving goals. To my daughter, Mildred D, who is an incredible example for me and who fills my heart with great joy. To Mrs. Carmen L who offered me her support and sent me in the right direction, thank you. To my friend Dr. Stephen A. Shechtman (doctor of psychology) for giving me strength through his educational examples. To my friend Dennis Grau, M.A. Psychology, CAC/CADC for being for me the brother that I never had. To Frances Dee, CAC/CADC for convincing me back in 1993 so that I could begin the journey for this story. To Joseph B for being a friend. To Bruce B, Ezequiel S., and Tina B. for their patience and the help given to me with regard to this manuscript, as well as the comfort and friendship they have all offered. To Mike "Sweet and Low because from you I learn something, and to my friend Edwin Alfonso B, my thanks to you also.. To my granddaughter, Derivette for her computer help and tutorials. To Joseph Braden for his help and friendship. To Jerry P whom with his support, friendship, and caring has remained in my life with great love. To my sister Iris Mirta V for her help and dedication relative to this project, thank you. To Mrs. Saida M for her work translating this manuscript from Spanish to English, my thanks to you also. To the founders of this program back in 1935 for the wisdom they acquired by the grace of God and for this 12 Steps which were more beneficial to me than the help of any psychiatrist. To the word "WE" with which I found the concept of unity, and my most sincere thanks to all of those people who throughout the years shared with me their constructive, positive examples. Lastly above all, thanks to God for bringing peace to my spirit One Day at a Time.

"Denial is the Truth that hurts when you don't see it"

Chapter 1 – My Childhood

My name is Ruben, and I was born August 13, 1954 in a small town in Utuado, Puerto Rico. Today there is no doubt in my mind that I was born sick at that time, and as the years passed, my emotional sickness progressed to the point of losing contact with the reality of life. Today it's not difficult to see those areas in my development where there existed constant personality insecurities, confusion, evil, lies, hate, and rage against humanity and God, as well as countless other mental maladjustments that afflict a human being daily, and those which we cover up with excuses so that we won't see ourselves as incomplete beings and to instead see ourselves as superior to others. My family lived a humble life, and under this humility, my father Andino and my mother Gladys Maria brought into existence three children, two of which were girls, and then me, the oldest boy. My mother was a woman of incredible beauty, and still today, I carry found memories of that beauty. I can't say much about my father, Andino, since I didn't have the pleasure of spending much time with him. However, in the few hours that I was able to be near him, and by listening to other people's comments about him, I learned of the deathly anguish that he lived with daily which today is called "alcoholism", and that which was the cause of his death in later years to come. Today, I can say that my father Andino was not a pleasant person when he was drunk, and usually, his behaviors were savage towards the people around him. It is a shame to have to say that most of the time, it was my mother Gladys Maria who paid and suffered the consequences of the savage actions of my father.

It is extremely important to be able to describe those details in my life which created a portion of mental anguish that for many, many years caused serious consequences in my existence. Under no circumstances do I wish to blame anyone or justify my sick behavior towards others, and the harm and pain that I caused. I only wish to establish that there is a great possibility that certain circumstances in my childhood contributed to my development of a healthy mind and with a certain amount of dignity.

There came the right moment in the life of my mother, Gladys Maria, in which she found herself forced to leave my father, Andino, and fight to re-build her life in the United States.

This part of my life has had a certain amount of obscurity in my development. It wasn't until too long ago that certain documents and photos from those years which had disappeared came into my possession. In the years when my mother Gladys Maria lived outside of Puerto Rico, she resided in the state of Florida. Today I have in my possession photos of those years when we lived in the United States. These photos that I have today tell a very painful story much later, but they are memories that have allowed this story to be told in its entirety.

I was four years old when these photos of my two sisters and me were taken, and they complete very painful memories of my life. At the age of four, my mother decided to bring me and my sisters back to Puerto Rico where we stayed in my Grandmother's house in Los Angeles De Utuado. It was there at my Grandmother's house that I remember having fun in a way that I had never experienced before. It was these memories from my childhood in which I can say there was a certain amount of happiness. Once again, after having spent some time with the family, my mother Gladys Maria decided to go back to the United States, but this time, she left all of us behind under the care of my Grandmother who was in charge of running this enormous farm where most of my fun took place.

This farm was an incredible paradise in which a child of my age could play and do his favorite pranks. Our home had a beautiful porch, and on the left side of that porch was "El Molino" (The Mill), that place where my aunt, my uncle and my Grandmother worked to process coffee beans. It was in this mill that the shell from the coffee bean was stripped away until the coffee bean was left clean, and once this was done, the coffee beans were dried and then handed out to customers so they could be roasted. While my family worked, I was free to play. There were very few toys in those days and to keep me busy, my Grandmother had given me a giant white female pig. This animal then became my favorite horse. Someone made a harness for it's mouth, and the old potato sacks became my saddle so that my back side wouldn't suffer too much damage when this sow would go wild "galloping" around the entire farm. Once my "horse" was saddled, the fun would start and climbing up on its back, I simply would give it a few taps with my small heels against its sides, and she would gallop all around. Usually, the outcome of my games had painful consequences for me for I was then "punished" by the low-hanging tree branches, and most of the time, I was thrown to the ground who always caught me as if it were waiting to cause me that very-well deserved pain due to my little adventures! When I look back on those years and/or that phase of my life, it brings me pleasant memories today.

It was also at this farm that I had the opportunity to encounter the brutal hand of my uncle. At that time, he was 13 or 14 years old and for his age, he was a fairly strong youth. One day, when I was using the bed like a trampoline, I experienced his brutality fall upon me. I had been previously warned that the beds were not made for jumping on them, but this warning fell upon my very deaf ears since I didn't put any amount of attention on it. Losing control over his actions, (my Uncle) proceeded to slam me against the wall that had two protruding nails that punctured my back upon impact. I was left with two large puncture wounds from which blood was quickly gushing out. The pain that this caused me was incredible, but my Uncle knew exactly how to pull himself out of the mess he had gotten himself into; just like so many other times, his lies always saved him from a beating by my Grandmother, and this incident for me became a very important lesson because I learned that whenever I did anything that was wrong, if my lie was a good one, that would take me out of the mischief that I had created for myself. This was a good lesson to follow the other teaching that I learned, and that was that the bed was not made for jumping on it. After this incident happened, it wasn't too much later that my Uncle decided to find his fortune in the United States where my mother was living. Once my Uncle left for the U.S., our stay at this farm didn't last long, and once again, my Grandmother became the person responsible for managing and maintaining another farm. This plantation had the largest coffee field that I can remember, and it covered the entire property and it made it seem as if the house was covered by the coffee trees. Here in this new home, I had a number of other experiences which caused serious consequences on my small conscience. Now that my Uncle had left, it was required that the young boy of the house fill in for him by picking the coffee beans. I didn't like this work since I hated the stupid canister that became a constant part of my person, and my time for fun had ended. I now spent my whole day going from shrub to shrub picking the detested coffee beans. My sisters were spared from this ridiculous work as they were much younger and they stayed at home while my Aunt, my Grandmother, and this servant spent the entire day from shrub to shrub picking the cursed coffee. At that time, my Grandmother was having a romantic relationship with my Aunt's father outside of marriage, and Don Jesus was a man who was limited in his mental faculties. In addition to that, he was very pleasant to deal with. He had a growth on the back of his neck and sometimes, he would ask me to rub his neck since this would alleviate the pain that he felt. When I wasn't picking the despicable coffee beans, I spent my time having fun with Don Jesus since his mental capacity was very similar to mine. At that time, I shared a room with my sisters and my Aunt, and in that room, I began to suffer much mental anguish due to unpleasant acts that consumed my conscience for many years to come. The amount of shame that I felt coupled with the mental confusion began to create very unpleasant results within me. Today, at the age of 55, I know how destructive sexual abuse is for people during their early development, and I also know the harm that it causes a human being throughout their life. I started to grow up as a mentally sick child who had an incredible amount of rage with everything that surrounded me, and my actions were destructive. One of those destructive acts fell upon the black cat of the house, and one day, after it had eaten one of the chickens from the coop, my rage fell on him. Behind the house there were two large metal drums that collected the rainwater which was later filtered to be used in the house. It was inside one of these metal tubs that I drowned that cat until his life force completely disappeared. The bad thing about this act was not that I took the life of that cat, but that I felt a great sense of satisfaction with this destructive act. Maybe you, the reader is thinking "How is it that this child at the age of six can still remember the amount of satisfaction that this incident gave him?", but I will continue by saying that I remember exactly that day as if I were re-living it today. However, with this new deed, more mental confusion

4

came into my life, and my small conscience began to experience a type of remorse never known before. With this act, there came another negative idea to my life, and one of those adult superstitions was that I was going to suffer seven years of bad luck, and that this bad luck would be the worst type of my life. I will tell you honestly that I witnessed that bad luck become a reality in the years to come. Today, I know very well that what happened in my life had nothing to do with superstitions or bad luck, but at that time, my innocence told me otherwise. It was required that I offer a burial for this animal whom I had taken its life, and I dug its grave across the street in the shady part of the fields across the river. I made a wooden cross and placed it at the head of the grave. I made sure to bury it across the river so that its spirit would not come looking for me. I believed that since water had caused its death, its spirit would be afraid to cross the river to come after me. Some time passed, and that black cat disappeared from my mind and memory completely, and I once again continued with the hated task of picking the coffee beans, something that I detested with all of my heart. However, I could not say no to this task since I was reminded of it by the whip that my Grandmother used on me; that this was an obligation for me, not a choice. In my mind, the whip carries many unpleasant memories since it had become my skin's best friend, and each time that I came into contact with it, the welts that it left on my body brought fear to anyone who saw them. There was another time in my life in which I experienced incredible pain that caused me grave consequences. While I was picking coffee beans, I felt the urge to urinate, and while doing so, I didn't realize that I was urinating on top of a beehive that had the wildest bees that you can imagine, and my small penis (which normally had to be found with a magnifying glass) had now completely shrunk into my body. I don't remember what happened next, except that completely stung, swollen, and suffering from excruciating and incredible pain caused by hundreds of bee stings, I ended up in the emergency room at Utuado hospital. The damage that those bees caused to my body was quite alarming and upsetting to my family, and this was another one of those experiences in which I had the opportunity to be in contact with my favorite best friend – pain. Time passed, and things went back to normal, and once again, that hated coffee receptacle became part of me again, but now whenever I went to pick the coffee, I was much more careful when picking a spot to urinate! Not long after that, my mother returned from the United States back into to our lives, and with her arrival there also came a new little brother. This child was the result of a love affair between Don Julio and my mother, Gladys Maria. My infant stepbrother had been born with a bronchial illness, which eventually led to his death a short time after arriving in Puerto Rico. After his funeral, my mother Gladys Maria decided to take me to live with her and she left my two sisters in the care of my Grandmother. Once again, I was happy because that stupid coffee receptacle had disappeared and I didn't have to pick coffee anymore. Now I could return to my favorite games and pranks, and I spent my time helping my mother with some of the household chores, although most of the time, my mother had to re-do much of what I did. One of the tasks that I was required to do was to get water from the river to wash our clothes, dishes and kitchen utensils. This task was a bit difficult for me since I had to carry a tub of water up a hill and by the time I got home with it, most of the water would spill since it was to hard for me to carry the tub, and usually, I spilled more than what I brought home! Realizing my problem, my mother, Gladys Maria, built a little cart for me that had a square box in the back where I could place the tub of water and this way, most of the water arrived intact at the house. I was very proud of her invention, and she noticed this. Not much later, she made me another toy from an old bicycle wheel. She removed all of its middle spokes so that now it was just a round hoop, and then she made a tool from a metal clothes hanger that I could use to run and roll the hoop around the fields. Until this day, I cannot forget the moment when my mother expressed her love by making those toys for me. Some time passed, and one day, my mother decided to wash the bedding. The sun was very bright and hot that day, but it was a beautiful day, and the song of the *pitirre* bird could be heard from afar, and it wasn't too long before she asked me to go to the river to get the water which gave me a chance to use the cart that she had made for me; this was the greatest fun that I could ever have for one day. At that time, I was seven years old, and whenever I helped my mother, I felt happy. It was on that sunny day when the song of the *pitirre* was present that I truly understood what suffering is and I experienced what pain truly means pain that in many instances almost cost me my life. Once I returned from the river with the water, my mother started to wash the bed sheets. I was tired from pulling the cart up the hill, so I sat on the steps of the front of the house to rest a bit.

While she continued her work, I was sitting a few feet away from where she was standing, and at that moment, we heard the sound of a car engine approaching the house. The road was at the top of our house, and it almost looked like the house was enclosed in a hole. To get to the house, you had to go down a path that was covered in grass and stone pebbles, and it was on that path that the biggest nightmare that my life has had at that time came, (but it was not the last) to arrived. Don Julio, the father of my deceased stepbrother, was slowly walking down this path; he seemed as if he didn't want to slip and fall. Once my mother saw him, she coldly greeted him, as if she really didn't want to see him. I stayed sitting where I was while they spoke. Shortly thereafter, the conversation turned into screams of rage, and Don Julio pulled out a nickel plated gun and began to shoot my mother Gladys Maria over, and over again until she fell to the ground. Once the paramedics arrived at our home and had pronounce my mother dead the white sheet she was washing on that day became her permanent shelter in her death. The number of shots that Don Julio fired upon my mother totaled six, and once the gun was empty, he tried to reload it again to continue shooting, but he dropped the bullets and then he started running down the same path he had arrived on and he got into a taxicab headed for the airport where he was later detained by the police. Once Don Julio was arrested at the International Airport in Isla Verde, he was tried and was sentenced to serve his time at the prison in Rio Piedras, Puerto Rico. There was a time in my life where I couldn't understand how it was that this man had the nerve to write to my Grandmother to ask about the well being of the three orphan children that had been left behind due to his savage behavior. Today I can understand why Don Julio tried to keep communication with my Grandmother through written letters. I imagine that the guilt running through his conscience must have been monstrous and hellish for him. However, by trying to improve his conscience with this, he did nothing good with mine since daily, it was becoming more out of the norm, in time, it became something so alarming and destructive just like the savage actions that he committed against my mother, Gladys Maria. I carried locked away inside of me this incredible hatred as the days and years passed. This drowned me daily in such a sad, tragic way that my life had become the most disagreeable that any human being could imagine. The funeral of my mother was something so painful for our family that the suffering that this incident created began to leave irreparable scars in our home. The first of these was when my Grandmother decided to allow one of my sisters to be adopted by another family so that economically speaking, they could offer her a better life and maybe with them, she could find the love and nurturing that my Grandmother would never have been capable of giving her. It has been many years since the murder of my mother, and still today, I do not know whatever happened to my sister, but I don't lose the hope of one day being able to sit with her and open up those channels of communication with her and her family for the rest of my life.

After my sister left with her new family, my Grandmother made her next decision which required that we move from this place that had caused so much pain to our family. We now started to pack our belongings to take with us the pain of this incident to yet another town in Puerto Rico. Once the moving truck took the road towards our new destination, *the hound of our home called "Whose Knocking?" jumped out of the truck and was lost deep within the farm, and with this came another familiar loss.*

Our new destination became Arecibo, Puerto Rico, and it was assumed that in this new place our lives would blossom with beauty and without misfortune. Yet my Grandmother was unaware of the ticking time bomb around her, and when it blew, the damage it would cause would be irreparable. An incorrigible child was growing up whom no amount of punishment could control, and my Grandmother's whip had become my loyal friend; it couldn't live without me, and Ruben could not live without it. It was as if one were created for the other. A rebellious child was growing who hated everything around him. This child had no respect for nothing or no one – the norms at home and at school were abused as he saw convenient. Once at school, I started having problems with the other students as they would make fun of the way that I spoke since my accent was different from theirs, and this brought to my life innumerable problems. I began to feel self-conscious and different from those other children, and these inferior complexes began to occupy a large part of my time. One day while our teacher was teaching our lesson for the day, one of the students received the punishment that he deserved for mocking the way I spoke. Gripping my pencil as if it were a knife, I stabbed him completely through the entire palm of his hand. Blood quickly started gushing out of the wound of his hand, and the teacher had to take him to the school infirmary. The results of this act brought serious consequences to me home for I was brutally whipped and beaten by my Grandmother. At that time, I was in constant trouble at home and I had taken on another bad habit – anything and everything that was out of place came to be in my possession. A little thief was developing who had no respect for the belongings of others. I remember as if it were today that my Aunt used to collect Kennedy half-dollars, and these would disappear from their spot quite often. As time passed, more disagreeable faults developed within me, and I was always in trouble at home. My Grandmother at this point in time worked tirelessly ironing clothes and cleaning other people's houses to be able to provide for us our daily bread. She worked very long hours and did her very best to provide us with daily food and a decent place to live, but Ruben had become a constant problem in her life. I was eight years old by this time, and once again, I found myself being sexually attacked by a much older boy, and once again, this caused within me a mess of negative emotions that for many years would continue making me feel uncomfortable, less than, or less of a man than others. For many years, I blamed myself and was filled with guilt and shame. With this new loathsome act there came a number of emotional problems that affected my life; I began to wet my bed daily, my nervous condition didn't allow me to eat, and the dirt beneath my fingernails became my daily sustenance. I was growing as a malnourished child who couldn't feed himself, and I was whipped daily by my Grandmother to force myself to put something to eat into my stomach. I had become the class clown, and I constantly sought attention by my bad behaviors, which continued causing me daily problems at home. My grades weren't too bad so I was able to graduate from San Luis Elementary School, and with this graduation there came a small amount of freedom for me since now I had become a middle school student, and this gave me the chance to do whatever I wished and wanted. Once I registered in this new school, my first day of class was celebrated with an incredible fistfight. I had to let all of the other students know that I wasn't going to take their abuse, and here was the chance to get some recognition at school; my attitudes were terrible, and my behavior was restless, and my stay at Jefferson was short-lived. I was soon expelled. My Grandmother didn't know what else to do with me because I had become a savage kid which no amount of punishment would control. It seemed that the number of beatings and punches I got didn't matter; I had become immune to them. Just before graduating from the sixth grade, my father Andino came back into our lives from the United States, and he was in bad physical shape while he continued doing what he knew best – getting drunk. At a bar, he came upon someone who wouldn't put up with his nonsense and this person proceeded to stab him numerous times. He was nearly killed, and his wounds were so serious that most of his vital organs inside of his stomach and his intestines had to be surgically replaced with plastic ones. It's incredible that despite being bed-ridden in critical condition at my Grandmother's home, my father's alcoholism still told him that there was nothing wrong with him and he continued to drink liquor as if nothing had happened to him.

My first contact with alcohol began during the time that my father Andino stayed with us. At that time, the wounds he had received did not allow him to move from the sick bed that he was confined to, and I was the one who would handle his errands to the store. There were many times that I found myself tasting the sweetened mix of anisette and Bacardi rum followed by that special warmth that this concoction gave my body. In that short time that my father stayed at my Grandmother's home, I began having some special fun times with my father because once he recovered from his injuries, he took me to visit my cousins and uncles who lived by the "Dos Bocas" river. However, once his wounds completely healed, once again, he disappeared from our lives the same way that he had come back. This was the last time that I saw him alive. My father Andino eventually suffered a violent death at the hands of some people who maybe like him did not know what alcoholism was and who were probably lost in that very same world that I also became lost in. The day that my father was murdered, I was playing basketball when I saw my Grandmother walking towards me, and I could see the pain in her face that she was carrying. Once she arrived where I was, she gave me the news that my father had been once again stabbed numerous times, and that he had died on route to the hospital in Arecibo. If I were to tell you that this news caused me pain and heartache, I would be lying to you because in my mind, I felt comfortable with the idea that he would never again hurt and cause pain to anyone because I held him responsible for my Mother's death even though he wasn't the one who pulled the trigger. His death didn't cause any pain within me for I felt I hadn't lost anything important in my life. It's a shame that he had to die in the violent manner that he died, and it's sad that he never knew about the disease of alcoholism and that he never had the chance to be freed from his self-imposed infernal prison which ended up taking his life.

Yet today, I can see the power that that liquid has and the destruction that it brought to my life and to countless other lives. I give thanks to my God for having freed me from the obsession that almost took my life to the same place in which my father ended up.

Once another tragedy came to our lives again, my Grandmother decided to move and we were now living in a project called "Marques Arbona." This place was more modern and had a basketball court where I spent most of my time. It also had a baseball park in which I played in frequently.

<u>Chapter II – Adolescence</u>

By this time, I found myself looking for the acceptance of a group of older guys who accepted me within their circle with no judgments or questions. With this new group of friends, I acquired some new habits, and other people's property would disappear as soon as I laid eyes on it. My favorite stores were those that sold expensive clothes because since I was poor, I had **extravagant/expensive** taste. I liked to dress well, and I knew that the girls liked guys that dressed in style, and it was a way to get them to fall in love. By this time, my Grandmother had met another man, and it seemed as if another romance would soon blossom. After seeing each other for a while, they decided to marry. Don Domingo was a Christian, and he had no idea of what was in store for him with me. Today, I know that even a good Christian could lose their mental composure when it pertained to me. It was incredible to witness the change that my Grandmother underwent being near this man of the Christian faith; her appearance became something astonishing. The lipstick that once used to adorn her mouth had now disappeared. The Chesterfield cigarettes that she smoked no longer existed. The beers that she used to drink were no longer found in the refrigerator. Her short dresses now became ankle-length skirts, and she never again wore a short dress or skirt. The statues, icons, and pictures of the (Catholic) Saints disappeared from the walls of our house, and we now had a new book of rules at home that were worthless to me. It was now required that I attend church on Sundays and Thursdays, and I constantly rebelled against this as I saw fit. My Grandmother, who had made these amazing changes and had taken this religion thing so seriously, would continue to lose patience with me, and she used to unload a mess of beatings on me to make me have some respect and force me to go to the church services. But this had no effect on me since I was immune to the abuse and mistreatment that I was constantly used to receiving. Once again, the time had come for me to return to school after having been expelled from Jefferson Elementary School, so my Grandmother registered me at the Jose Gualberto Padilla school in the Cotto *barrio* in Arecibo; it was considered a "hot" neighborhood. This was where I would start the 7th grade. I was often in trouble at this new school, but my grades were fairly good. My addictive habits by this point had escalated – the inhaled use of paint remover, paint thinners, and other toxic glues (Ross/Testors) kept me in that dark place where I felt good about myself because I hated who I was. My life wasn't worth even two black pennies, and Bacardi rum, gin, and beer relieved the pain that was so deeply ingrained within my soul. What existed was an empty shell that hated everything around it. My sick behavior kept me in constant fights since my low self-esteem and my sick attitudes didn't allow me to see the reality of my life. I had become a repulsive and unpleasant individual with everyone around me. I often found myself in trouble with the law, but I was always lucky to be able to get away with it. Now I was entering my adolescence, and my Grandmother had given up on me since she couldn't figure out what else to do with me because it didn't matter what amount of punishment I received – I did exactly what I wanted whenever I wanted. I would often run away from home, and while I was away from home, I committed all of the scandalous acts that I felt like because there was no one who could or would control me. I had become a hoodlum who had no type of respect either at home or with society. By 1969, I ran away from home again and I ended up in San Juan, the capital, along with two other friends with whom I took this adventure. Like me, they were tired of the monotony in their lives, and once we found ourselves in San Juan, the difficult task started. We had no place to stay, and we didn't have a single penny to feed ourselves. My friend Danny had previously lived in that area, and he know how to fixed the situation. He had once worked in a restaurant there called "El Okuizan" and it was here where we found some work. Our other friend, Alf, decided to go back to Arecibo for once he found himself hungry and homeless, his heart filled with terror. Until this day, I still don't know exactly how he returned back to Arecibo, and I have never asked him because we still remember the stupidities done under what is termed "mental insanity". During the time that we were at 18th Street in San Juan, we slept wherever we could – on the beach, in abandoned houses and buildings, but it was usually in one particular abandoned house that was close to the restaurant so it was easy to get to work in the morning. I had become a kitchen helper and I had multiple tasks to do: I peeled potatoes, cleaned the floors and the dining room, was a busboy and washed dishes while my friend Danny just loafed around since he knew the owner better. The owner knew of our situation and that we were living at that abandoned house, so every once in a while, he would take us to his house so that we could clean up, change our clothes, until shortly thereafter, he allowed us to stay in his home. However, this arrangement was short-lived since one day, Danny was accused by one of the waitresses of stealing her tips, and the owner became furious at all of us so he threw us out back out on the street. Incidentally, the situation didn't end there since Danny had already made a plan to get back into the owner's house to rob and ransack it and take whatever we could find. We waited for the right time, and breaking in through a window, we searched the house from top to bottom until we found the money that he kept saved to buy the daily food supplies for the restaurant. He had the cash stuffed in four separate socks which promptly became part of our "belongings." We knew that once the owner returned home that night, the police would be looking for us, so we decided to return back to Arecibo. Looking back on this, it's amazing for me to see how ungrateful and selfish I was, and just how much of a destructive of a person I had become, and how unpleasant my behaviors and actions were at that time. Once back in Arecibo, I went back to my Grandmother's house, and it seemed as if no one had returned. I heard no arguments, and no one asked me any questions about my whereabouts. It was as if my Grandmother had convinced herself that my life was unworthy of being "saved". I gave her a few dollars of the money that I had left, and she never once asked me where it came from. It was as if nothing about my life interested her. Once again, my friends and I began planning our next escapade, and our friends from "El Cotto" *barrio* now gave us all of the attention we were searching for because we wanted to feel superior to all of them, even though inside, we were full of fear due to what we had done in San Juan. We managed to convince the father of one of our friends to try and get us plane tickets to the United States. He said he would help us if we would also pay for a ticket for his son who had become a headache to his family and he felt that this was the best way for them to get rid of him. Danny and I had decided that it didn't matter if we spent extra money on another plane ticket. The important thing was to get out of Puerto Rico, so we agreed to do this. The day before we were scheduled to take the flight to the U.S., we decided to have a street party on 3rd Street in El Cotto. The Bacardi rum and the beer showed up as always, and once we drank enough alcohol, things again got out of hand and the "wars" between us started. I did not realize the damage that the cursed drink was causing me, and I found myself plunged into this giant garbage can that had become my daily life. This behavior was our way of living life, and I remember having vowed to myself that I would never become like my father, but with each moment that passed, I became more exactly like the very thing that I hated. There were many days that my mental state wouldn't allow me to get to my house to sleep, so the street became my bed for the night. The day finally came for us to take our flight, and I don't exactly remember when we got to the International Airport in Isla Verde since I was in really bad physical shape from the night before. The wait at the airport seemed to take an eternity. It was time for us to board the plane towards our new destination in Brooklyn, NY. I felt a bit emotional since I was unable to say goodbye to my Grandmother and my mind was racing like crazy. Once the plane took off from the runway, it wasn't long before I fell asleep and I woke up as the flight attendant was starting to serve some food and beverages. We passed the rest of the flight time by talking and joking about non important garbage. Now the **Captain/ pilot** was announcing that we were approaching Kennedy airport and we were told to fasten our seatbelts for the landing. It was then that I saw one of the most awesome images that a youth of my age could ever have seen – in the distance, all of the city lights were lit up in the beautiful night scene, and it seemed as if the plane was about to land in a brilliant field of sparkling diamonds. However, I could not have imagined the surprise that I was to get much later once I arrived in Brooklyn. My friend Rey spoke perfect English, but Danny and I didn't understand much of it. We got to Brooklyn, and my eyes beheld another incredible view. There were burned buildings, stripped and abandoned cars in the streets, and there was garbage thrown everywhere along with drunk people stretched out in the doorways of these buildings. It was as if we had landed in the biggest garbage dump that I had ever seen. The vision of sparkling diamonds that I had just experienced had quickly vanished, and I found myself yet in another slum like the ones that I had seen in Puerto Rico. Once we arrived to Rey's brother's house, Danny and I were expecting that we would have a place to stay. Yet once arriving there, as we were being introduced to the family, we discovered how small and cramped this apartment was and how uncomfortably these people lived. Nevertheless, I didn't care if I had to sleep on the floor, but sometimes the things that we plan don't always turn out as we expect, and if you don't have a backup "plan of attack", we usually get mentally lost. That's what happened the minute that Mary, Rey's sister-in-law, set eyes on us. Seeing three more mouths to feed apart from the three that already lived there, she lost control and started verbalizing her annoyance and her feelings to her husband without caring who was present to hear her. Watching her starting to lose her temper and sensing that she was getting ready to go into a rage, Danny and I immediately understood that we were not welcome there, and we had no choice but to quickly leave this place. Now we had to start thinking about what we were going to do next since we were in a strange country, we didn't know the language, we knew no one else, much less how to get from point A to point B. Fear started to grip me, but never once did I let Danny know what emotions I was feeling because "real men" don't show their emotions to other men. After taking some time to think, Danny explained that we had to ask someone how to get to the Bronx since he was sure that once we found his sister's house, she would let us stay there. Once we decided what to do, we did just that and it wasn't too difficult because someone told us how to take the Q/J train to Delancey Street, and once at Delancey, we should take the Number 2 train to Simpson Avenue in the Bronx. During the subway ride, there were many moments of worry and doubt, and at times, panic would take hold of me but eventually, like so many other times, things eventually fell in place. Once we arrived to Danny's sister's house, again I found myself rejected because she told him that she was willing to let him stay there, but I had to leave because she did not want to become responsible for me since we were not related, and she had no idea what type of person I was. Suddenly, things had gone from bad to worse because now I was being tossed out on the street like a garbage bag that no one wanted. While leaving that house, I became mentally lost, and the tears started trickling quickly down my face as I felt a horrendous fear creep within me; I didn't know what to do with this situation. Once I gathered my thoughts, I decided to go back to Brooklyn and do battle as best as I could. I went back to Rey's neighborhood, and I concocted a plan to get the help that I needed. I remembered that Rey spoke English and with him, things would probably go better for me. However, I also knew that this wasn't my worst problem. My biggest problem was that I was homeless and on the street, and I had to find some decent shelter for the night. Once I arrived where Rey lived, I decided to walk to the garage where his brother Angel worked as a mechanic to ask him where Rey was. He pointed me in the direction that Rey was headed, and I followed in that direction where I eventually found him. He was with a bunch of young guys that he knew from before when he had lived in the neighborhood, and he introduced me to them. They all greeted me as if we had all known each other before. They all had strange names. One of them was called "The Cowboy", and he was filthy. He looked as if he hadn't seen a bath in centuries; his shirt collar was black with dirt and grime, but he seemed quite happy with his appearance. There was another guy named "Stuff" and he was Puerto Rican. They were in a gang, and they called themselves "Satan's Angels", and these litte "angels" had control over a large part of the narcotics sale and drug trafficking at that time. These gang members were prohibited from speaking to me in Spanish because they wanted me to learn English. They gave me the nickname "El Jibaro", and once again, I felt the same complex that I felt when the other kids at school would laugh at my accent. But these guys were different. They only wanted to help me to understand what they were telling me. The dreams and ambitions of these young guys had been lost in the giant garbage can that existed around them, and it seemed as if I was also beginning to get lost inside that same garbage that surrounded me. These guys lived in an abandoned building, and it was their club. There, they sold heroin, **marijuana/pot** and anything else that people wanted. This place became my home, and when I didn't stay there to sleep, I slept in the back of a milk truck that was parked behind the garage where Angel worked.

At that time, heroin was the product that addicts chased, and this substance had started causing**?? chaos ??** in my life. It was mid 1969, and I had managed to become addicted to this incredible drug which controlled all of the deep pain that I felt within my soul, and my inferiority complexes disappeared once this poison entered my veins. I had become a pathological liar who started believing his own lies, each one bigger than the last. I manipulated people exactly as I wanted with the motive of getting whatever Ruben wanted to stay in the state of darkness where I felt comfortable. I used my lies in such an amazing way that the people who heard them were so moved in their hearts by what I said that they gave me exactly what I wanted without a problem. It's astonishing to look back and see the type of person that I had become; I couldn't see the constant harm that I caused every day. I was full of excuses for everything, and I justified my behavior by saying that if you would have witnessed and experienced what I saw, you too would be doing what I did. In Brooklyn, I had started to live a sick lifestyle that I was already used to, and I had no problem finding what I needed to survive. My friend Rey by now had found a job at that same garage where his brother worked, and Ruben had now become a drug dealer. A bundle of smack cost $21, and individual bags were sold for $3 or $4 dollars. The drug dealer always got his own share with each deal. Each tablespoon was worth about $60 dollars, and once the dealer cut the product with Quinine, the percentage of what he earned was good because usually, a tablespoon was 1/7 or 1/8 of a cut. By this time, my addiction had grown enormously, and I was usually short with my cash drop off. "Vasi" who brought me the product, was usually understanding and he didn't complain much about the $3 to $4 dollar shortages. Once in a while, I used to pass by the gas station, and acting as if I was helping out, I would steal from the gas pumps to feed our habit, for by this time, Rey had also started using. But I didn't know that this party wasn't going to last long because the owner of the gas station started to notice that something was wrong with **the displays** on the gas pumps, and knew that somebody was stealing the money. "Madame Heroin" had become the owner of my life, and she dictated each move and action I would take. I often found myself selling more drugs to make more money so that I could shoot more heroin. It was as if my entire life revolved around this cursed substance. During this time, we were living at a couple's apartment, and they had no idea what was going to befall them. Once the husband Jose tried a little bit of this drug, his marriage crumbled until his wife decided to leave him, and now we completely controlled Jose and his home which had now become a drug den. His house was the neighborhood "pharmacy" and the steady stream of people who came and went was constant. New problems came with all of this because the narcotics officers knew what was happening at this spot, which meant that the house would be soon raided. The day that the detectives picked to shut down our operation, the house was full of addicts buying their "medicine"; we usually didn't sell to you if we didn't know you, and that was the rule. But on that day, we missed one and we sold to someone whom we had not sold to before, and he passed me some marked bills. The sale wasn't large, but the detectives had to shut down the "pharmacy" since this was their job. Once the front door was **forced/busted** down, the real problems started. "Vasi's" girlfriend was there with us. The detectives were interested in finding the product that we had which was difficult for them to find because I had removed the suction cups from the bottom of the dining room table legs, and I had hidden the "stash" of drugs inside of the hollow table legs. The detectives tore the house apart from top to bottom, and the rage they had was incredible because they couldn't find the drugs. Losing patience, they began slapping me so that I would tell them where the drugs were with no results. They took another approach and started interrogating the others present; there were only four of us there – Rey, "Vasi's" girlfriend, my drug connection (and the addict who had paid me with the marked bills), and myself. They separated all of us and took us into different rooms for questioning, and after a while, they handcuffed me, "Vasi's" girlfriend, who was my connection and they took us downstairs to the squad car. They released Rey and the other drug addict. Once inside the police car, we rode for about 20 minutes, but the detectives knew where they were headed. Once we pulled up to and apartment building, they pulled me out of the car and led me up the staircase to an apartment that had a number 7 on the door. They knocked on the door and the owners asked who it was so they answered "Vasi" and the occupants opened the door not knowing what was awaiting for them. Once inside, the detectives did what they knew how to do, and their discovery led to finding seven or eight bundles of heroin, scales to weigh the product, baggies, and a bunch of other items that they would probably use to add to the list of charges. "Vasi's" girlfriend was still handcuffed inside of the squad car which was parked in front of the building. I also was still handcuffed inside of the apartment along with the other people who were inside at the time of the bust. The detectives were happy because their work had paid off and they had some good results. Once their work was done, "Vasi's" girlfriend and I were no longer important to them. For a long time, my friend Rey talked a lot of trash about what happened that day when the detectives released him, and he made statements that could have cost me my life, because one of the main rules is that a "rat" has no one's forgiveness; you never snitch. Those are the codes of the street, and when you're involved in any illegal activity, you have to learn to put a zipper on your mouth. I know quite well that "Vasi's" girlfriend use to go with him to pick up the product, and I also know that when the detectives took me to that apartment building, it was because they had the right information. Once we were freed, "Vasi's" girlfriend went home, and I continued with my destructive way of life at the young age of 14. I had become something destructive and unpleasant, and I tried any and every type of substance available as long as it always took me back to that dark place in which I was submerged. I weighed about 85 pounds by this time, I was once again suffering from malnutrition, and I was still sleeping in the streets and stealing whatever I could to support my habit. It was more important for me to have my "cure" than it was to eat.

Winter was quickly approaching, and one day while searching my wallet, I found a little piece of paper that had a faded phone number. I decided to dial it to see who it belonged to, and much to my surprise, the number that I had just dialed was for my Aunt's house that lived in New Jersey. This made her immensely happy since the family had given me up for dead since they knew nothing about my whereabouts. After a few minutes of talking, I explained my situation to her and without refusal, she offered me her help and gave me her address and directions to get to her home. She told me to take bus # 99 from Port Authority on 42nd Street until it arrived to Stevens Avenue in Jersey City. After walking a few blocks, I found myself at her front door ringing her door bell. Once she set eyes on me, she got a tremendous shock because standing before her was a walking cadaver. My hair was beyond shoulder length and my physical appearance left lots to talk about. Now began the difficult task of detoxing me from this deadly, cursed addiction that I had. The first 72 hours was pure hell – the vomiting and diarrhea were excruciating, the sweating was constant and profuse, along with chills, shakes, and pain in my entire body and joints. I could hardly stand it, but that's how I survived almost a week of pure hell. Once my body started improving, there was yet a greater pain to be endured – that of the mental obsession. After staying a few months at my Aunt's house, she decided to buy me a plane ticket to go back to Puerto Rico and once I arrived at my Grandmother's house, she again "welcomed" me with a new book of rules which I told her that I understood hoping that I could just get her off my back and not have to listen to her lecturing.

It was now the mid 1971's and one of the rules of the house was that I was to return to back to school once again at Jose Gualberto Padilla in the "Cotto" *barrio* of Arecibo – the very same one that I had quit to go to San Juan. Once my Grandmother registered me, the Principal explained to me that the students whom I had started the 7th grade with were now beginning the 9th grade. If I managed to get a "B" average in half of the 8th grade course work and a B in half of the 9th grade course work, I would be able to graduate with the 9th grade class. I knew that they were doing this to get rid of me, but by this time, it was the best deal that I had, so I decided to start paying attention to my studies one hundred percent. Once the moment of truth arrived, I managed to graduate with honors. I remember that day as if it were yesterday. The graduation was held in the San Luis theater, and once my name was called and I was given my diploma, it seemed as if they had awarded me a medal for all of my efforts. However, this event couldn't change the truth, and this was that the drink, the glue, the paint remover and any other junk that I could use to take me to that place where I felt good about myself was still the escape that I was looking for as a way to get out of that pain which I still felt so deeply within me. While I was going to school, I met a girl who became interested in me, and I also was interested in her, so we began seen each other frequently. However, Alma did not know what she had come to know, as it was easy for me to act like a chameleon for her to see me as a whole person, although inside, I was an empty shell. Once I graduated 9th grade, I started my freshman year of high school, and as in past occasions, I again celebrated my first day of school with a major fistfight trying to defend a friend who had **physical problems/was handicapped** (??)Once again, I found myself back in the Principal's office listening to his lecture while he told me that if I didn't change my attitudes and my behavior, he would have not choice but to expel me from school.

"If you don't love yourself, you have an enemy for a friend".

<u>Chapter III – As An Adult</u>

It was now 1972 and my friends were enlisting in the Army, which seemed to be a good idea. So, we went by the recruitment office, to take the exam, and now we were being sent to Fort Buchanan to **pledge the oath,** and once this was done, our next stop would by Fort Jackson. But before leaving, I told my Grandmother about my plans and she was overjoyed with happiness! I, on the other hand, was thinking that now I would be able to visit all of those places that I was used to seeing on TV and that I had heard other people talk about but that I knew nothing of. Yet, before leaving for Fort Jackson, I had to let my girlfriend Alma know about my decision; she seemed to be a bit saddened by it, but eventually, she accepted my decision. I explained to her that I would keep in contact with her by mail and that once I arrived at my permanent post, I would request a pass to then travel to Puerto Rico so that I could ask for her hand in marriage. Now, after having said goodbye to my friends and my Grandmother, we held a tremendous party in the plaza on 3rd Street, and the drunk that I caught that night was disastrous. Now the time came for us to leave for San Juan to board the bus that would take us to the C-141 plane bound for the military airport in South Carolina. This was a new experience for me, and I kept in mind that I had wanted to do something constructive with my life because I was tired of my way of living. But I had Forgotten that it didn't matter where I went – I always took my worst enemy with me, myself. Here at Fort Jackson I began Basic Training and while we were in training, we weren't allowed outside of the base and were confined to certain areas. Nevertheless, this had no importance for me since Ruben did whatever he wanted; I would "escape" from the barracks and go out to the bar to find that liquid that my body now craved: alcohol. It was more powerful than I, and I wasn't worried about the consequences that I would have to pay as long as I could pour this marvelous liquid into me. During the time that I was stationed at Fort Jackson, I was incredibly lucky because I never got into any trouble. Yet, once my basic training was done and they sent me to Fort Sam Houston in Texas to AIT, it wasn't very long before my use of alcohol and later heroin would begin causing problems for me. By this time, I was studying to become a paramedic but it seemed as if I was rarely happy unless I found myself in that mental darkness which was so comfortable for me where I felt no pain inside of me. The beast that lived within me had now escaped and it was very difficult to tame it; I was full of excuses for everything, and the self pity that I felt for myself was incredible. I was constantly running around with different women and I swore to myself that I was the best thing that existed in their lives. My false machismo, my Pathological lies, my false pride, my insecurities, they all created their daily destruction within me; the sad part of all of this was that I was deeply convinced that I was better than everyone else around me. The truth was that I felt full of hate and rage which kept me in a complete and constant state of mental insanity. Here at Fort Sam Houston, once again lost in my mental darkness, I continued with my physical, mental, and spiritual destruction as I had done in the past and my life was a complete disaster. I proceeded with the alcoholism that had taken my father to the grave, and now the addiction to drugs had totally taken control of me. It didn't matter to me what substance I put in my body as long as it "worked." Once while I was inhaling a liquid called "Carbona", it caused me to lose my mental faculties and I passed out. Once I regained consciousness, I found myself strapped to a bed in the psychiatric hospital of that military base. Once I was released from that hospital and was back at my post, my fellow soldiers told me that after I inhaled that toxic liquid, I bolted and took off running through the barracks until I jumped out of a window falling 40 feet until I hit the ground. But my problems didn't end there. Now I was being investigated by several Federal Government branches where I was accused of attempting to defraud the United States government by trying to make them believe that I had lost my mind and maybe this would allow the chance to sue them for Veteran's benefits. At no time were these ever my intentions, and until this day, I still suffer from permanent physical damage due to the impact of that fall on my spine and my back. The incident was due to the effects of having inhaled that "carbona" liquid on that day. The interrogation that this military branch conducted against me took them to the conclusion that the information that I had given them had been appropriate and they all agreed after some time that it would be more convenient for them to transfer me to a different training program altogether. After a few weeks, I received new orders for another military post in Fort Polk, Louisiana. Here at this new base, I was going to start my new training in culinary arts until I could graduate and become a cook. Yet, it seemed as if it didn't matter where I went – alcohol and drugs were once again present in my life and problems would once again reappear just like they had in the past. By this time, Mescalin, "window pane" acid, four-way purple microdots and "black beauties" kept me in total mental obscurity where I just existed without caring what was happening around me. Now that I had graduated from culinary school, new orders were issued for another military base in Fort. Benning, Georgia. It was here that I began my parachuting training and while I was at this school, alcohol and all of the other garbage that I was used to consuming were still in my life daily. Once I graduated from parachuting school, orders were again issued for my new permanent post where I would begin working as a military cook. This would be the last military base where I would complete my remaining service time on my military contract. Yet, once those orders arrived for this permanent post, I was able to request from my superiors a military leave pass so that I could visit my Grandmother and my girlfriend in Puerto Rico before starting that next assignment. Once my pass was approved to visit my family and my girlfriend, I started making plans for my trip. I made the flight reservations and left everything in order for my return to Fort Bragg. I felt satisfied in this new post and I kept my appearance and my military equipment in working order at all times. My military ranking at this time was Specialist, Grade 4 and I though I was being considered for a promotion to a Specialist, Grade 5, this would never come to pass. I started feeling a desire for a possible career in the military and in making plans for my future. I kept in mind that Alma was going to become my wife and that I wanted to have a home of my own – something that I had never had before. I had good plans in my mind, but I didn't know how to implement them. Once my leave was approved and everything was in order, I traveled to Puerto Rico and once I had boarded that flight, I opened my bottle of Valium and I ordered a few small bottles of Bacardi. I took three or four Valiums and washed them down with the Bacardi without a second thought. I realize that the plane was scheduled to make two stops at two airports, but until this day, I still don't know where it was that it landed because once I found myself again in that darkness, nothing else seemed important in my life. The flight landed at the International Airport en Isla Verde, Puerto Rico, and I found myself taking a taxicab bound for my hometown in Arecibo. Once I arrived at my Grandmother's house, she was filled with joy because standing before her was someone whom she thought was different. Yet, at no time could she imagine who I was inside. The neighbors gave me a warm welcome and they treated me with a certain kind of respect because they believed that Ruben was becoming a young man and what they didn't know was that the person who stood before them had not absolutely changed at all. My Grandmother then told me that my girlfriend Alma had visited with her often and that it was only proper that I pay her a visit at her house. With no further discussion about this, I left to go to Alma's house. I had taken a few Valiums to help steady my nerves because I was thinking that this would probably be the day on which I would ask for Alma's hand in marriage. Once at Alma's sister's house, Luna, her sister, welcomed me with a certain amount of kindness yet I feared that as Alma's older sister, she was not going to readily agree to my marriage proposal to her younger sister. However, once Luna gave her consent for her sister to marry me, we started making our wedding plans. We were approaching the end of 1973, and during the time that I had enlisted in the army, I didn't have a single penny saved since all of my pay had been spent on alcohol and the use and abuse of other controlled substances. This was both a destructive and vicious cycle, which I couldn't end. Once I returned back to Fort Bragg, I started my cooking duties and while I worked, I made plans to return to Puerto Rico to marry Alma. While all of this was happening, my addiction was progressing more out of control every second. The town of Fayetteville had become my second home and once in this new place, my destructive life took free reign. I swore to myself that I was a tremendous "Casanova" and I would use women as I pleased as long as I got whatever else I wanted, be it sex, money, drugs, or alcohol. My values and morals were in a deplorable state, and the worst part of all of this was that I was blind to this truth, and in plain English, this is called "DENIAL" – a word that describes the state of my entire life. On March 29th, 1974, Alma and I decided to get marry, and I remember that my finances were in such a bad condition that I had to take out a loan to buy Alma her set of wedding rings and some of the other things that we needed for our wedding. On this very special occasion when two people were going to undertake this marital union before the sight of God, the groom didn't have enough courage to do so. When my brother in -law came by my Grandmother's house to pick me up for the ceremony, I wasn't even dressed. My military uniform was hanging in the same spot from when I first arrived at my Grandmother's house, and he then knew that something wasn't quite right. I felt terror inside, but I couldn't let him know that because "real men" don't have fear. I had four purple microdot tablets on me, and this was a very potent type of acid. When my brother-in-law saw what I had, he wanted me to give him a piece of that microdot, so he took half of a tablet, and I took one and a half. Now I finally got the courage that I needed to proceed with this wedding. The date was March 29th, 1974 and Alma was about to become Mrs. Alma S. She was quite beautiful in her white wedding dress, yet Ruben was out of control and on another planet. I started "tripping" on this drug and the hallucinations were starting to create a horrible panic within me. The marriage ceremony had already started, and I couldn't comprehend any of the very important words that make this union so special. The photographer had starting taking pictures, yet every time the camera would hit my line of vision, my facial expressions in those photos said a lot before the eyes of all of those wedding guests. It wasn't long before my brother-in-law lost control of himself and his actions became so repulsive that his family was forced to remove him from the ceremony, and I think that he was later taken to the hospital for medical treatment. After the minister completed our ceremony and Alma and Ruben had been joined in holy matrimony, the wedding cake was cut and served, and once the reception ended, we left for our honeymoon. The wedding had turned out fairly well, somewhat modest but at the same time, quite pleasant and Alma was very happy. But Ruben was lost again back in that dark mental obscurity in which I didn't feel the emotional pain that I still carried within the depths of my being. Once we arrived at the hotel to start enjoying our honeymoon, that acid that I had "dropped" earlier that day before the wedding was still causing chaos within me and I had no desire to fulfill my conjugal duties. Instead, I found myself inside of a bathtub immersed in a bubble bath playing with soap bubbles with my mind completely lost again like so many other times in the past. It's true that until this day, I still can't remember if in that very special moment within a marriage whether or not I had the chance to make love to my wife Alma that night. However,

I can tell you that during the years we were together, our marital relations were always quite enjoyable and pleasurable. It's amazing that our friendship has remained throughout all of those years of separation. With this marriage, more emotional conflicts started to appear within me. Before having married Alma, I had arranged for the military to take out $150 dollars a month out of my pay to be sent to my Grandmother and now after this marriage, this money was now going to be passed onto my wife which was not to my Grandmother's liking. This issue and the war that erupted because of it left me feeling more full of rage while at the same time feeling an incredible amount of guilt within me. I watched the only person left in my family place their greed before the happiness that I felt with Alma. After our wedding and once things were settled as best as they could between my Grandmother and I, we decided to leave to Brooklyn, NY thinking that we would stay only a few days to visit one of Alma's other sisters before continuing on towards Fort Bragg, North Carolina. I can't recall if at that time Alma ever noticed my mental state Because I always tried to hide my use and abuse of controlled substances, as well as my alcoholism, although most of the time, I was not really interested in her opinion or comments. I found myself living in a cycle of disease which my wife eventually also became a part of. We later found ourselves constantly getting drunk together, and the use of acid made our sex relations even more passionate and hot, or so we thought! It wasn't long before the physical and verbal abuse left violent scars in our marriage which eventually deteriorated quickly. Towards the end of 1974, I decided to re-enlist for four more years. At that time, I knew that Alma was pregnant and that it was my duty to secure a future for our family. But as the days passed, I became a more and more irresponsible person. On January 29th of 1975, Alma found herself alone at the hospital in Fort Bragg giving birth to our daughter Ruby while I found myself at a hotel in Fayetteville playing the "Casanova" with another woman. By the time I got to the hospital, Alma had already given birth. My daughter was beautiful and I felt an amazing happiness within me. However, despite all of this, my behavior was still as unpleasant as you can imagine because I continued running around with other women and using whatever chemical garbage there was around to be able to face life. There were many occasions in which the other women that I was spending time with would have to drag me to the front door of my house because the horrific drunk that I had tied on wouldn't allow me to get home on my own. My marital infidelity was causing a disaster in Alma's life and one could see the deep daily emotional pain that all of this was causing her. At the same time, I was having a secret affair with a native Cherokee woman who later became pregnant and the only solution that I could come up with was to send Alma away to her sister's house in Brooklyn. This way, I thought that I could continue to have the freedom to do exactly as I wished and wanted. My addiction was increasing daily in such a way that my military tasks had started to deteriorate and I often found myself in the Captain's office getting cited under Article 15 due to the problems I had caused myself. By this time, my mental state was out of control. I had bought a .32 caliber hand gun and whenever I went to Fayetteville, I always carried it with me. My life was out of control and on a few occasions, I held people up at gunpoint to take their money and belongings. I was running around with another addict known on the streets as "Madera" (Wood), and once, I almost killed him with a beating. The day before I beat him with the shotgun, I had bought a color TV for my wife Alma as her birthday gift. and "Madera" and I went to pick up the TV and brought it back to my house, but he waited until I left for work one day and he broke into my house and stole my wife's birthday gift. The rage that this created in me was immense, and once I told my other friend, "Rodriguez" what had happened, he helped me to search for "Madera" throughout the town of Fayetteville until we managed to find him in the company of his girlfriend. I then proceeded to hit them both and forced them into a car and we drove to my house. Once we got there, I handcuffed "Madera" and proceeded to beat him within an inch of his life. After some time of suffering by my repeated blows, "Madera" then told me where he had taken my wife Alma's TV set. So, we took him and drove out to the place that he directed us to, and he went inside and re-appeared with the TV set after some time. When I had held "Madera" and his girlfriend both hostage at my house, I had also taken from him a "Luger" pistol which I kept for a very long time. When I look back at my actions done in that dark past and I think about all of the laws that I broke while committing my insane behaviors, I realize that God has been extremely great in my life and that he has saved me from my own self-destruction. I wish I could tell you that my savage acts and my erratic behavior would have begun to change by that time, but this would be a lie because for many more years, I became my own worst enemy and the destruction that I brought into the lives of the people who loved me and even to those that I didn't know was one and the same. After Alma and my daughter Ruby went back to Brooklyn, NY I thought that things were going to get better. But this would become a very difficult task because my problems began to increase more and more daily. By this time, I was having problems in the dining room with my kitchen Sergeant; and if people of color accuse whites of being racists, then so in that way, today I can say that colored people also have their share of racists. There are some things in life that one learns in order to live in this world, and while I was living in Puerto Rico, I had never experienced the level of soul sickness and racism that exists in the United States in which I have lived in almost all of my life. Yet, I do remember having attended school in Puerto Rico and having had the opportunity to interact with other children who like myself had no concept of what racism was. But this story is not based on the sickness that exists in the world and the malady of the mind they have but on my own mental deviations. Now that Alma had returned, I found myself in trouble with Sergeant Davis; I had to find the way to resolve the mess that I now had on my hands. My lover and mistress "Anne" was pregnant, and I had to conceal this relationship up until the very end, as I didn't want my wife Alma to find out what was happening. My superiors had given me orders for more military training at West Point, New York which would mean that Alma and my newborn daughter Ruby would have to stay alone in north Carolina until I completed this training exercise. So, I started to pack my military equipment and all of the items that I would need for the cadet training, and once we arrived at West Point, I unpacked and properly stored all of my equipment where it belonged and then I started looking for a way to get over to the town of Newburg, NY to begin my destruction. During the time that we were at West Point, I had a verbal disagreement with Sergeant Davis which eventually escalated and got out of control. It seems that sometimes these people of color usually play a very unpleasant game called "The Dirty Dozens" and Sergeant Davis had the indecency of dirtying his mouth with the memory of my deceased/murdered Mother which for me was the worst type of disrespect and an unforgivable insult. This caused me to lose complete control of myself and I threatened to kill him in the presence of a number of other people and this caused me a very serious problem and consequence. After our military exercises were done at West Point and we were heading back to Fort Bragg, it was usually required that my military unit grant me three to four days of leave to spend with my family. However, Sergeant Davis, in order to punish me for what had happened at West Point, decided instead to send me out on yet another military exercise. This then raised within me a horrific resentment towards this man, and once again, I found myself packing up my equipment and sorting out all of my belongings and packing those in their respective bags. I made sure that I also packed my bottle of Valium and two or three pints of Bacardi; I then called my wife Alma to tell her what had happened. Now I found myself heading out on another cargo truck to yet another jungle to play little soldier games! Once we arrived at our destination, all of the kitchen equipment had to be unloaded from the cargo trucks and we had to set up tents and organize all of the dining room equipment. Sergeant Davis knew exactly how to "punish" me by assigning me one of the dirtiest, messiest tasks in that kitchen. I was now responsible for cleaning out the emerging heaters and receptacles which held all of the dishes to be washed which once cleaned had to appear shiny and spotless. Once I had cleaned and placed everything back in its place after completing my task, I walked out and found two trees where I hung up my hammock so I could take a break. I then took four or five Valiums along with my pint of Bacardi and I went into that familiar darkness in which I found myself daily where everything seemed so different for me. But it wouldn't be too long before Sergeant Davis would arrive at my rest spot to disrupt/ disturb my peace of mind to then take me to a place where I would become his worst enemy. Until this day, I can't remember exactly what Sergeant Davis said or did to me for me to transform into the savage that I became. Yet, I can remember exactly when I got hold of the ice pick that I had nailed into the tree trunk where my hammock was tied to, and I remember clearly having plunged it into his stomach using every ounce of strength within me. Once I stabbed that ice pick into his stomach and he felt the pain from the stab wound which I inflicted upon him, terror grabbed a hold of him and he turned around and started running away while I repeatedly continued stabbing him in the back several times. He collapsed to the ground after running a short distance as I attempted to take his life. I truly wanted to kill him by any means necessary, but the other soldiers in my unit jumped on me to subdue me; once they had me locked down and under control, my superiors explained the consequences that I would be facing for my actions which at the time didn't matter to me. Nothing they said really registered in my mind. Once the MP'S had put me in handcuffs and took me into custody and we were headed out to the military prison, out of the corner of my eye

I saw when Sergeant Davis was placed on a stretcher to be taken by ambulance to the military hospital. While still handcuffed, I jumped out of the jeep and started running in the same direction as where he was; the jeep was traveling at about 25 mph and when I dropped to the ground, the gravel on the road dug deeply into my knees and my face, but that didn't matter to me. The only thing that mattered for me at that moment was that I wanted to end this man's life no matter what the cost. Once I was again subdued and picked up again by the MP's and locked up in prison inside of my cell, my complaints and sorrows started taking control of me. Once my mind awoke from the darkness that it was in and I started to realize the seriousness of my situation, fear overtook me since I believed that what I had done would carry grievous consequences for me. Not once did I even think about the wounds that I had inflicted upon this man and how my false macho bravado had taken over. Yet, my comments to the other inmates were very grandiose because I wanted to be seen as someone important in this place. After spending a few months in this jail cell, the military provided me with an attorney to represent me in this case and the defense that he provided me was impeccable as all of the pending charges against me were quite huge. Among the few of them were attempted murder, aggravated assault, illegal possession of a weapon along with countless others that all carried many years of jail time. While I was incarcerated, my wife Alma would visit me as often as she could and she found herself confused as to what to do about our marriage. I thought that I might be imprisoned for years so I thought it best that Alma start thinking about making a future life for herself and my daughter Ruby and forget about me altogether. Meanwhile, my mistress "Ann" was also pregnant and this secret was eating me up inside because I didn't want to cause more pain to Alma than I had already caused her. I know today that I'm only as sick as my secrets. Yet at that time, I already knew that my marriage had already ended and that the only thing that I could do was to wait for my sentence and move on with my life. I also thought that Alma had no one to help her and this truly bothered me deep inside. One day while she was visiting me, Alma told me that the Red Cross had offered to help her to return to Puerto Rico and I was glad to hear that since her problem had been resolved. This would be the last time that I would be able to speak to Alma since once I was sentenced, I would lose contact with her for some time. Once my trial started, my attorney used all of the details that I had given him of my life – my mother's murder, my father's death, and countless other details – to paint a picture of mental sickness. I believe that his strategy worked as my sentence turned out to be to serve out the remaining time that I had left on my re-enlistment which I eventually served at the prison in Fort Leavenworth, Kansas. However, it's amazing to me that under no circumstances did I ever feel any remorse for the savage acts that I had committed against Sgt. Davis, or the pain that I had caused to Alma with my actions. I also didn't care that "Ann" was pregnant, and that my continual rebelliousness was often still causing me problems. In one particular occasion, I was involved in a riot in the dining room which brought me more unpleasant results and with this latest incident, new charges were brought against me and I found myself on trial again for aggravated assault. I was then transferred from population to maximum security and remained incarcerated there, while in maximum security i received a letter from "Ann" telling me that she had lost the baby after falling at home; this did cause me some pain not so much because she had lost the baby, but because now I would have no place to go once I got out of prison since I knew that Alma and I were a thing of the past. The selfishness within me was of the most unpleasant type that a human being could display, but for me, it meant nothing as I was living in a darkness outside of this world. Once again, I had been absolved/cleared of the riot incident and the charges of aggravated assault; I thought I had gotten away with it because I knew how to manipulate the system since I was "smarter" than everyone else. After serving about nine months in maximum security, the time was approaching where I would be freed, and I had been told that I had to find some clothes to wear on the day that I would be released from prison; I found some through a mail order catalog. I ordered a bright yellow terry cloth jumpsuit/warm up suit, a pair of black platform shoes, and a black "Frenchie" cap – this was the outfit that I would wear to return back into society!! I had now saved up enough money which would give me a new beginning in the street. The day that I was finally released, the temperature in Kansas City had hit 102 degrees, and the heat index was brutal. I found myself at the airport with all of this money in hand and once again, self-pity took over me and I justified my self by telling me that I "deserved" to have a few drinks since the government had "stolen" part of my life with this years of imprisonment. Once I got to the airport bar, I told the bartender to get me a Bacardi and Coke and to keep them coming until further notice. This was another one of those times when I had the chance to experience what a blackout was – something that I would again experience in the future on many other occasions. It was now 1977, and once my flight was ready to depart and they announced boarding time over the loudspeakers, all of the passengers began boarding the plane; I knew that with this trip I wold leave behind a few years of my life which would never return back to me again. Now, already bound for New Jersey and the beverage cart went by, I continued along with my destruction as I had always done in the past. It was incredible to me that in just a few hours I had returned back to that time in which I almost took Sergeant Davis' life with my aggressive attacks, and I didn't realize that my denial kept me in complete mental darkness. Yet, I did not know that this disease of alcoholism is progressive and fatal at the same time. Once the plane landed at Newark Airport, my new life would begin. I had no other clothes or other personal belongings with me. The only thing I had with me was the money that I had saved up during my incarceration. Once I got to the airport terminal, I headed towards the Exit where I knew that my Aunt would be waiting there for me with her husband. I sensed that as I walked out towards the Exit, people were probably laughing as they spotted me walking, yet I didn't realize that they were laughing about my appearance since I looked like a yellow canary and a black splotch on top of my head!! Yet, I swore to myself that I looked like the "coolest" dude in that entire airport! I think I probably lost about 10 pounds during that long walk wearing that heavy jumpsuit which was suffocating me, yet my Aunt and her husband welcomed me with affection as we drove off towards their home on Stevens Avenue; they now had moved to a larger house. However, it wasn't long before my alcoholism would begin to cause problems in my Aunt's life and in her marriage. On many occasions, I found myself in arguments with her neighbors and I would become abusive with them and others, so much so that once, while I was attacking one of her male neighbors, he defended himself with a knife and in order to avoid worse problems, my Aunt simply paid for a plane ticket and sent me back to Puerto Rico. Once there when I arrived back at my Grandmother's house, I again became the worst nightmare in her life. I know very well that this woman suffered with me as never before since in a short time again, I was arrested again and went back to jail in Arecibo under the charge of receiving stolen property. That night when I was arrested, I had started "partying" early, and around midnight, I decide to go "help" my friend who worked at a gas station since he had told me that once we got the work done, we would go out and get a few shots of rum which actually never happened. Suddenly, one of my other friends pulled up in a car with some other guys and they invited me to go drinking with them instead. They then showed me a bottle of gin, and in my defiance, I couldn't think straight, so I decided to leave with them to finish the "party". Before I got into their car, however, my friend from the gas station warned me that this wasn't a good idea, but I didn't listen; I just got into the car with "Daly", "Melo", and "Black " as we called him, not even thinking or caring about who owned the car they were driving. But at the end of that night, I became better informed about this because of the consequences which I later had to pay that revealed to me who the owner of that car really was. Once we started getting drunk, we drove around and crashed a wedding, caused trouble and were chased out. On the way back to "El Cotto" barrio, the driver of the car decided to turn the car around near an embankment overlooking a cliff but he flipped it instead, and everybody except for me jumped out of the car because the car went over the cliff. I stayed behind unable to get out since I was pinned in the back seat with the gas from the gas tank dripping all over me. Once the police arrived and they pulled me out of the overturned car, they hit me a few times and took me in handcuffs to the municipal jail. Later on, the owner of the car that had been stolen filed charges against "Dely", "Black", and myself. According to "Blacks" recollection of this incident, "Johnny", the car's owner, had been trying to start the car earlier that night, so "Black" came by and while pretending to help him get the car started, he instead took "Johnny" for a fool and somehow managed to get into the car and drove off with it and stole it from "Johnny". If I had listened to my friend while I was back at the gas station, none of this would have happened to me.

Once "Black" and "Daly" were released on their own recognizance, they were both worried because the only one of us who had a clean record in Puerto Rico was me since I had never had any serious trouble on the island. Yet, I ended up pleading guilty to the charges and my two friends were set free. The time that I spent in the municipal jail wasn't long and they transferred me to the penitentiary in Sabana Hoyos where I was able to post bail and continue right along with my insane merry ways! It wasn't long before I found myself back in trouble. This time after a long binge of non-stop drinking for days, I stabbed myself in the chest a few inches away from my heart; I recall the blood gushing from the wound prior to my setting fire to my Grandmother's house. The police quickly appeared on the scene and once I was handcuffed, I was taken to the psychiatric hospital *in rio piedras* where Thorazine (SP??) became my best friend. Before having stabbed myself, I had often been planning my own death since I hated my life and everything around me. Now I found myself locked up in a ward with other mental patients; they would often urinate over me and their bodily excretions would cover my body since my weakened physical condition didn't allow me to get up from the floor. After spending some time in this hospital, once the doctors thought I was improving, they allowed me to go outside for some recreational time, and on one of these "excursions",I escape from this place. Out of all of the hospitals in which I found myself admitted for psychiatric treatment during my lifetime, the psychiatric hospital in Rio Piedras Puerto Rico has been one of the most repulsive and unpleasant one in which I've had the chance to waste my time seeking medical help. By this time, my depressed state was such that I only wished that death would soon arrive and thus put and end to the deep pain that I felt. My nerves were in such a horrific state that when I walked, my entire body would shake and tremble uncontrollably; my head seemed to be constantly gesturing to the world "NO" as the shaking was so intense. Now that I had escaped from this hospital, I didn't have a chance to stay out on the streets for long because soon again, I found myself admitted to yet another psych clinic, and while there, things improved a bit despite having the doctors use me as a guinea pig to find the right medication that would manage my condition. After some time of being locked up while under treatment, my Grandmother eventually came to visit me during a weekend; she had brought me divorce papers as my wife Alma had decided to end our marriage. She picked the best time to do this and I can't blame her for wanting to get rid of the person that I had become since I was now an invalid and it would have been a shame if she would have to wasted more years of her life living with a person like me. Once the doctors thought I had reached a more stable mental state, they released me from the psych clinic. Yet, once I was returned back to my Grandmother's house, I again found myself with the pint of Bacardi in my hands which I drank and mixed with my prescription medication which produced in me a very unpleasant mental state. I found myself drugged up daily and my drunken bouts were horrendous. I had lost an entire year trying to find improvement of my mental state and yet in only a few days back at my Grandmother's house, I had returned back to that deplorable state of living. It was now mid-1978 and once again, Ruben had decided to run away from that person who was his worst enemy and it never mattered where he went because his "nightmare" was always present there with him. After having decided to return to New Jersey to my Aunt's house, I had the opportunity to meet the sister of my Aunt's husband; this young lady had a certain resemblance to my ex-wife, Alma. They were both the same height, and she more or less resembled Alma a bit. Yet, I know quite well that she could have never imagined that to her life there would be arriving the greatest hurricane ever. Today, after many years of being apart, I know very well that I felt no real love for her, but I also know that being with her was comfortable for me since I had found yet another woman who endured my abuse and tried as much as she could to help me with my problems. When I mention that it was "comfortable", I mean to say that after having been incarcerated in a Federal prison and having spent all that time seeking psychiatric help while having been alone for such a long time, the companionship of a woman was like a pleasant, amazing treasure. "Bebe" is an incredible woman and I know that her only wish was to have someone in her life who would give her the love that she deserved. But, how was I to give her something that I knew nothing about since I had never in my life been able to receive it? It's very difficult to give someone something which you've never had since you don't know anything about it. "Bebe" was 18 years old when I met her, and her brother knew exactly the type of person that I was and he wasn't agreeable to my courting her. Yet, it wouldn't be too long before our relationship would begin to grow. She was also pregnant and the young man who had impregnated her did not want to take any responsibility for having done so. But for me, this wasn't a problem since I had accepted what had happened and I was willing to help her once she gave birth. This young woman had numerous incredible gifts and qualities. She was friendly, kind and caring and with her, I thought that I could get what I didn't have with Alma. It had been a few years since I knew anything about the whereabouts of my daughter Ruby, and here with Bebe I would have another chance to make a home. Bebe was living with her Grandmother, and this lady took a liking to me; she had a certain affection for me, and although Bebe,s brother disapproved of our relationship, this sweet woman offered us her utmost support. After telling her about our plans, she helped us and we decided to find an apartment and Bebe and I began living together. Today I thank God for not allowing Bebe's Grandmother to witness the damage that I caused her granddaughter in the years to come because I know that learning of all of that pain and suffering that I eventually had caused Bebe would probably had taken her life. On June 25th of 1978, Bebe was admitted to New Jersey Medical Center in order to give birth to my daughter Millie. This time, I was physically present to witness her birth something that I couldn't do when my daughter Ruby was born back in Ft. Bragg. By this time, we had a nicely furnished apartment and I felt happy since I now had a family – something that always meant so much for me as it was something that I never had in my childhood. However, it seemed that it never mattered what I had in my life because I didn't have the capacity to be grateful for my blessing and I would usually sabotage whatever I had in order to always have something to complain about and thus, I could continue feeling sorry for myself. As the days passed, my alcoholism and my addiction would again begin to cause more wreckage in this new relationship, and Bebe would be the one to pay the consequences with my verbal and physical abuse, and she would take all that she could withstand trying to get the love that she wanted. The police was called to our door on numerous occasions because I would usually destroy everything in the house or because I would physically strike Bebe and her injuries would require her to seek medical treatment. My blackouts were constant and I found myself jailed several times and waking up in a cell not knowing what had happened or why I was locked up. By this time, I was running with a gang of people who did not value other people's life and our behavior was of the worst kind, quite violent and most abhorrent. I had become a savage who didn't care about anything or anyone, and the only thing that mattered in my life was finding my drugs and alcohol. Outside of that, nothing held value for me and I didn't care who paid the consequences as long as I got what I wanted. There were so many times where I would find myself imprisoned and I would serve at least one year only to be released again to be arrested again and I'd serve two years, get back out on the streets and follow the pattern again; I would subsequently experience this battle for about 13 years of my life. I could probably spend an eternity telling you more unpleasant stories and describe in detail all the times that I hurt Bebe physically whether it was because I was in a blackout or because due to my rage in that moment had to come out and she would have to pay the consequences. Maybe her love for me was what made her able to withstand the tragic and sad conditions that she lived in; or maybe it was because she thought that she would be able to "save" me from my own self-destruction. Yet for whatever reason, today I don't believe that anyone deserved the type of life that I gave to the mother of my children during the years that we were together. In 1979, Bebe's Grandmother passed away and this left a huge and incredible void with in me since this lady had given me the affection that my own biological Grandmother never knew how to give to me. This death caused me a great deal of pain. The funeral was held in Puerto Rico and once everyone came back to the States, things began to get worse for me. Once again, I felt alone and abandoned and it seemed as if all of those people who gave me their love were always torn away from my life since I felt that I didn't deserve for anyone to love me. Bebe didn't know how to treat me since my complexes and insecurities continued their daily destruction in our lives and thus under all of this suffering, under all of the fear and abuse Bebe was still willing to make this all work. It was now 1980 and on April 18th, my son Ruben, Jr. was born. I still remember the day when his mother and I conceived him; I was still under the effects of another horrific drunken bout, and while I was making love to his mother, I later remembered having told that God that I didn't believe existed in my life that "if you are so great and mighty, why don't you give me a male child who can carry my name?" I had forgotten that "demand" that I had made until much later, but God did not forget. Many years later, I remembered that so-called "prayer" that I had made to that non-existent God in my life who had not been there on that bright sunny day when you could hear the birdsong of the "Pitirre" bird which was the one day Don Julio had chosen as the fateful day to take my Mother's life. Today, I have no doubt in my mind that God grants you those prayers that you make, and in the same way that He grants you blessings, He will also remove them from your life if you don't appreciate them. I know quite well that when He removed my children from my life, He did so with the purpose of saving them from the destruction that I would have caused in their lives. Eventually, my son Ruben, Jr. and my daughter milly began to grow up in a home where my mental insanity was starting to leave its imprint on their development while I found myself still in complete darkness about that issue. My children witnessed the physical abuse that I vented against their mother, along with the fights with the police. They also saw when armed drug dealers would appear at our house looking for me because I had stolen their product/or beaten them. They witnessed when I brought other addicts with me to our home to get high. Yet with all of this, I know very well that God protected them from all of this sickness and devastation. In 1981 while under another fit of mental insanity, I was home alone trapped in a deep episode of self-pity and mounting insecurities which had grabbed a hold of me. Bebe, as in many other occasions, had already packed up the kids and left the house running for their lives since she knew all to well what was going to happen once I had cracked open that first beer; it was best if she and the kids just weren't around. It was a Friday, and I had stocked our house bar with different types of liquor. I had bought two cases each of Heineken and Budweiser beer, and two gallons each of Bacardi and gin. I had also bought some champagne since I was planning to throw a great party, and now I felt embarrassed because Bebe had ruined my plans and I couldn't find just the right story to tell the people that I had invited over for that night. Once I opened that first beer, I unleashed the beast that I was to become and I set him loose on the run; by the end of that weekend, I had trashed absolutely everything in that home. I had torn apart all of the bed mattresses and had broken off all of the legs from the chairs. I destroyed the living room furniture including the couch and the television, as well as all of the kitchen plates and glasses. It looked like a hurricane had literally roared through the house and when I awoke from that blackout, I was on an airplane bound for Puerto Rico and I couldn't remember anything that I had done that night. I had a shopping bag with me and inside, I found a few shirts, a pair of underwear and a pair of dress pants. I must have looked like a mental retard as I was wearing a T-shirt, a pair of shorts and some summer sandals; it was snowing when I had left New Jersey!! Today when I reflect back on all of the sacrifices that Bebe made in order to give my children the best of everything that she could, I still feel an enormous regret within myself as today I can see all of the hard work that she had to go through to ensure that our children would grow up with healthy minds. However, the damage that I caused while intoxicated and the people who suffered the consequences of my behaviors would always carry the scars of the pain that I caused them. Yet, the only person responsible for all of this insanity is me. From 1977 to 1989, I found myself in very dangerous situations where I was close to physical death on numerous occasions. I have repeatedly overdosed on heroin and cocaine, I have attempted suicide many times, and have even been involved in several gun shootouts with drug dealers. The repeated blows and beatings that I received from police have left their imprint on my body, and my numerous stays in mental hospitals leave much unsaid. However, I have never visited a more disastrous place, and I have never been in a prison that was greater than the prison that I created for myself inside of my own mind. There is no greater hell than the one a human being can create for himself/herself within their own being. By 1983 most of my "friends" from the world of addiction had started to contract the AIDS virus. Yet for me, this didn't mean much because I was still looking for death in whatever form possible. I usually found myself in the shooting galleries that addicts would use to "cure" their pain starting from 125th Street in Harlem running into lower Manhattan, as well as the galleries in New Jersey. Inside of the apartments, they would place a glass of water on top of a table which contained several syringes, and for a mere $2.00, you could have your pick of any disease you wanted. It's a real shame for me to have to recount these things, but I hope that perhaps my story can open the eyes of anyone who might find themselves lost in their life just as I was lost in mine and that maybe by identifying with some of these experiences, they might get to the place where I am today. As I said before, most of the people that I hung out with had contracted the AIDS virus but kept it a secret since they were filled with hatred against the world; they wanted to give that disease to anyone else without having a burden on their conscience. There were many times in which I found myself even sharing needles with some of these people who had the virus. By this point, I had already contracted Hepatitis B twice, Hepatitis A once, and towards the end of my run, I had contracted Hepatitis C. During the time that I was buying heroin in Harlem, the drug dealers at the time were using "meat tenderizer" to cut the drug which was slowly over time disintegrating my insides. The stench that emanated from my pores was quite repulsive. Yet, my wife Bebe continued to stay by my side always trying to get me back to a state of "normal" health. The doctors treated me with a serum for the Hepatitis B as well as Veroca A Plus vitamins for the Hepatitis A and little by little, I began to physically improve. Yet mentally and spiritually, I was still lost. It was now the beginning of 1987, and Bebe couldn't withstand/tolerate me anymore, and our marriage had reached the last knot of the rope; she had taken out a PFA against me and I couldn't be within 1,000 feet of Bebe's house or I'd face arrest. I was now living with another female addict who had the AIDS virus, and it was easy for me to manipulate her and use her for my benefit outside of the bed as well as in the streets. She spent most of her time prostituting herself and working the streets to support our drug habit, and we stayed together for some time. However, anyone who didn't know her could never imagine that this woman was sick with the AIDS virus much less be a prostitute as she was incredibly beautiful. Yet after living with Lori for quite a while, she eventually got tired of supporting two addictions, and she kicked me back out to the street. Now I found myself sleeping in the backseat of an abandoned VW Rabbit parked on Bartholdi Avenue in Jersey City. After a few weeks of sleeping out in the streets, I called Bebe to see if she would maybe allow me back into her house to at least shower and shave with the promise that I would quickly leave as soon as I was done. However, deep inside I knew that once she stood before me and took one look at me, she would agree to let me in the house on those terms since I knew that she didn't want anything else to do with me. It was now the beginning of 1988, and after some thought, Bebe started to explain to me the conditions that I would have to follow if I was going to be allowed to stay in her home again, but with this decision, a terrible nightmare returned once more into Bebe's life. I had admitted myself to an outpatient Methadone clinic where I would get 90 mgs. of this poison daily and once I mixed that drug with some Bacardi, I found myself back again in that comfortable darkness where I would continue to spend most of my days. It wasn't long before the blackouts and the violent rages returned, and under one of those episodes, I tried to cut Bebe's throat as I held a knife to her jugular vein and threatened her life. In the struggle that ensued, she cut her hand trying to get the knife away from her neck, and I found myself coming to in a jail cell the next day not knowing what had happened. Somehow, my stay in prison wasn't too long and I was released a short time later only to be imprisoned again after that experience. I had been living at the shelter on 12th Street in downtown Jersey City after I was released from jail, and it was there that I almost took the life of another fellow resident. On the day that I beat this man with a wooden two by four, my day at that shelter had started out just the same as every other one. They would wake us up early, feed us some Farina, and by 7:30 a.m. every morning, they'd release us from the building out onto the streets to go out and do whatever we pleased. In my case, it was to go out and get to the Methadone clinic where I would get my Adavan, Elevil, and my 90 mgs. of Methadone and then head out to the train stop on Grove Street where I would stand around and pester and panhandle the hard working taxpayer/working class citizens of the neighborhood so that I could go out and get my pint of Bacardi or Georgi Vodka to complete the blend that would take me back to that familiar, numb, and comfortable state of mind. That night returning back to the shelter, I suspected that they probably weren't going to let me back into the building since the gatekeeper at the entrance had previously warned me many times about not returning in a sober condition. When I got to the front door, I encountered the resistance that I already expected, but after a while of crying and begging to be allowed back in to get some much needed sleep, I was admitted back into the shelter. The night before, however, I had a problem with another resident who was also staying there at the shelter and I had decided that I wasn't going to allow taking any more abuse from this person, so I found a wooden two by four out in the street and I had brought it back upstairs to the shelter with me. That night, after we exchanged some harsh words and a problem began between us, I simply went and got a hold of that two by four and I proceeded to unload numerous amount of blows upon this man's head and body until he ended up in a critical state and I ended up locked up again, and this time, things didn't look good at all for me. When I beat this man unconscious, there had been about 15 people present in the room who witnessed the assault and they gave the police details of the event which in turn led them to be selected as witnesses against me once a trial date was scheduled. Yet, as in so many other occasions, after spending several months incarcerated, the day finally came when I would present myself to the Judge. He first told me exactly what he thought of me and then told me that if the victim whom I had assaulted were to die as a result of the injuries, that I would be facing a long term prison sentence, possibly even a life sentence. Once I was back in my jail cell, I called my wife Bebe and I told her what had happened, hoping that she would help me get some bail money. Yet she, under a justifiable rage, told me exactly what she thought of me, and then she asked me if I had already forgotten that I had tried to slice her throat or was I crazy?? There was no way that she was going to bail me out and that I was just going to have to work this out for myself as best I could since that was not her problem! As I hung up the phone and walked back toward my cell, I sensed that the hallway was semi-dark and I felt a horrific rage since I now knew what I had done at this time. Today when I speak of this incident, I do so because deep in my heart,

I am convinced that God hears all of those heart-felt pleas, and if you truly believe, He does grant them. I don't want the reader to think that I'm talking to you about religion since I don't consider myself to be a religious person. I do consider myself to be a spiritual person who although imperfect, tries every day to do the best that I can to be a decent human being with other people, something which in my past would've have been a concept from another planet. Once Bebe refused to help me, I looked down that semi-dark hallway and I heard when out of my mouth came these words, "God, help me, I'm tired of living this way. Please help me…" I wish that I could tell you that I heard His voice and that the earth moved, but nothing of that sort happened. I can tell you, though, that suddenly, all of those witnesses that were lined up to testify against me disappeared, and that the person that I had assaulted came out of the critical state and eventually recovered. When it came time to go back before the judge for sentencing, there was no longer any probable cause against me since the victim could not remember who exactly had assaulted him. As I stood again before that judge who had previously told me that he was going to lock me up for life, I heard him utter the words that would grant me my freedom once again. That was the last time that I found myself in a court of law. My God heard my prayer once again, just like when I asked him to give me a son while making love to Bebe while under the influence of that horrible drunkenness; once again, God came to give me His help. He didn't do so on the very day that I asked or during the next day, but when He thought that the weight of my suffering had been sufficient, and once He thought it was appropriate within His time frame, then and only then did He grant me my freedom. Maybe further along in this story I will explain little by little the things that I must do on a daily basis to stay away from my own self destruction and from those things which caused so much pain in my life and in the lives of so many other innocent people. I know very well that our God has a purpose for everyone in this world and it is within you to find it since no one can bring it into your hands. The belief and the faith I have today in my God had never before existed within me. But please don't thing that just because God doesn't physically manifest himself to us that this means that he doesn't exist. I can feel the air even though I can't see it which tells me that God is the same – I can sense Him even though I can't see Him. Against all odds, I'm not supposed to be alive today; I should have died many years ago given my self-destructive choices. Yet, I will tell you how I see things today. When I was shooting up heroin and cocaine and sharing needles with my friends who had AIDS and I was not infected -- that is a miracle in my life. The Hepatitis C that I suffered from is not longer detectable in my body; that is a miracle in my life. Once while involved in a shootout at the projects in Curry Woods, New Jersey, I was standing about six or seven feet away from the person that I was trying to kill, and after shooting my gun about five or six times, the gun I was holding somehow chewed up the bullets; I could have been imprisoned for the rest of my life for attempted murder or murder And thus, I could continue speaking of hundreds of instances in which I have seen God's love working in my favor. Sometimes we human beings can't see the blessings that God gives us since we spend our lives complaining about the things that we don't have instead of being grateful for the blessings that God grants us on a daily basis. That was the way that I used to be during most of my insane life until I got to where I find myself today thanks to my God. We already know that towards the end of the 1990's I had spent my last day in jail, and since that time, I haven't found myself in trouble with the law. Maybe you understand that this only happened because I no longer pour alcohol or any other garbage into my body. I also imagine that once you start to understand my story, you might also come to understand that it would have been very difficult for me to accomplish any of this on my own. Throughout the years, God has used many people who possess different types of knowledge in their lives as teaching tools for me to learn many lessons in my life today. It's impossible for me to take credit for other people's knowledge. But I will tell you that today when I hear some one who speaks with some good sense and is living a proper life, that person holds a special place in my heart. That's how Mrs. Carmen L is for me. I know very well that I can use her name since she gave me much needed support just at the time that I needed it the most. Mrs. Carmen L is an educated woman as well as very caring and kind; she offered me unconditional friendship when I truly needed a supportive friend, and with her, I found the beginning of a journey on which I'm still traveling along this path today. She gave me the encouragement to begin to see what I had done with my life, and it was she who gave me the strength and hope to begin to live a different life. Dona Carmen was the coordinator of a community agency in New Jersey called P.A.C.O. They sponsored a number of community programs including Meals on Wheels, housing assistance, drug and alcohol counseling, and AIDS education to name a few. While working here as a volunteer, I started to develop a foundation for my growth which later helped me to get a permanent job at this agency. This gave me the chance to start to feel useful once again, which in turn helped my self-esteem to grow. Yet along with this new-found personality change, my ego, pride and grandiosity started to grow right alongside and eventually it grew out of the norm which caused me some problems which could have been avoided. But I'll talk about this more later in order to outline some areas of personal growth that sometimes can become diseased. In the same way that Mrs. Lopez was instrumental in my physical, mental and spiritual recovery process, there also were others who helped me in this life process. Two of them were Miguel and Raymundo; thanks to them, I find myself where I am today in a totally different place from that dark and desolate existence where the emotional pain controlled my existence, and alcohol mixed with other substances only gave me a temporary escape. Once I was freed by the State of New Jersey in October of 1990, my first five days out on the streets were not very easy ones. For the first few nights, I found myself sleeping inside of a carousel in a small park back on Bartholdi Avenue. I was usually awakened by the policy who would very quickly let me know that they didn't want me there. By November 2nd, I found myself back on Ocean Avenue on my favorite corner sitting on top of an overturned garbage can waiting for someone to walk by who might have some money that I could take away so that I could go and start again on my path of self-destruction. However, God had other plans for me, and instead of sending someone with money, He sent salvation to my life. Miguel and Raymundo were two guys who just like me had suffered for many years from this disease of alcoholism and addition and they ran the streets of lower Manhattan right along with me, in addition to every other filthy corner around New Jersey, looking for that poison that was the catalyst in the daily destruction of our sad lives. If either one of them would have told me on that day when they arrived on that corner of Ocean and Neptune Avenue exactly where they were thinking of taking me, I would have told them that they were crazy; and I probably would be dead today. Yet when Raymundo parked his new truck on the street in front of my favorite spot where I was waiting for the next victim of the day, I could have never imagined that my life would eventually become what it is today. At that moment, my sick mind was telling me "You're ship is in!! You're going to go get trashed, and it's not going to cost you a thing." This was the way that I was always used to think. When the guys told me to get into their truck, I never thought that I would end up in a church basement listening to other alcoholics talking about what their former lives were about and what their lives had become. For the first time ever, I heard that alcoholism is a disease and that it can be arrested on a daily basis if you don't take the first drink or that first beer. They also explained that you can use the same technique with any other substance(s) that I may be using or abusing. When I got to that meeting, I found myself seeing other people that I had lost contact with throughout those insane years. They were laughing and they seemed so happy; it was something that seemed so strange for me since   I didn't know what it was to smile or be happy. As I mentioned before, those first few days out on the streets were not easy since living on that carousel on Bartholdi Avenue was not what I really wanted for my life, and once Raymundo and Miguel took me to that meeting, I heard what I needed to hear to continue along my journey so that I could get to where I am today. I will tell you that for someone who had no skills to face life on a daily basis, this was going to be a very difficult task since once one is used to living by running away from life's situations by looking for excuses to drink and to use drugs, it's very difficult to accept that you are the problem and that you don't have the power to stop using. My first two weeks of freedom were the most turbulent weeks of my life since I had to find shelter in a shooting gallery where alcoholics and addicts were constantly drinking and using drugs, but I had no other choice before me at that time; it was starting to get cold outdoors and I needed a place to stay. In this place, there were daily temptations around me and many offers were made to me every day by these people; I knew that they just wanted to have some more company to indulge in their misery since none of them really had my well-being in mind.

They simply wanted to see me back inside of that daily suffering where they still existed. But now, I knew that there was a Different way to live and it had been explained to me to try this solution for 90 days and if I didn't agree that this was a better way of life, I could go back to my past life and my misery would be refunded. The plan sounded good to me. Meanwhile, Raymundo and Miguel fought day by day to give me some of the knowledge that they had freely received which was working for them. Reymundo had about 18 months clean and Miguel had about 14 months clean which for me was astounding since I couldn't remember when in my life I was ever away from those substances not even for one day, and if I was ever away from them, it wasn't by my choice but because the State had me locked up in jail. At this point, I had about 20 days without using, and one Friday night at my group, I raised my hand and shared about everything that was happening with me. I told them about my living situation and I didn't leave out any details. Once the meeting ended, two guys approached me and told me that they were renting a house and that they had an empty room and if I wanted, that I could move in with them. Felipe had about two years clean, and "Fat jim" as we used to call him had about 18 months. Now, I need to mention that just because they had the amount of clean time they had without using, it didn't mean that they didn't stop being alcoholics and addicts since this disease never sleeps, and if one is not vigilant, there is a chance that it can come back to take over your soul once again. One Friday night around 6 p.m. while I was getting ready to attend that very same meeting where Raymundo and Miguel had taken me the first time, Felipe came back to the house with a bundle of heroin. While I was in the bathroom shaving, I heard a loud crash in the kitchen and when I went downstairs, I found Felipe passed out on the floor from a drug overdose; there was a syringe next to him and on top of the kitchen table, I saw the spoon and the two bags of heroin that he had just injected. Nevertheless, this was nothing new to me because I had witnessed incidents like this numerous times but I knew that I had to do something to help Felipe. After struggling to help him get out of that state of unconsciousness, I called an ambulance as his lips were starting to turn blue and the light from his eyes was fading, and I knew I couldn't do much more for him. Once the police and the paramedics arrived, they started working on resuscitating Felipe. Yet before they got there, I had already cleaned off the table and had stashed the other eight bags of heroin that Felipe had bought to avoid more trouble. Somehow I was able to provide the police with a reasonable explanation and they seemed satisfied with my answers. After they left with the ambulance to take Felipe to the hospital, I headed out to my meeting. Once we started our discussion, I raised my hand and shared about what had just happened at the house with Felipe and people gave my their suggestions on what I should do about the stashed drugs. But the truth is that my disease was telling me a bunch of crazy things, the first one being that if I used one of those bags on myself, no one would have to know! But the other part of my mind told me that I would know and I remembered saying to myself, "Ruben, you're only as sick as your secrets..." and I swear to you that the hour that I found myself battling with that disease seemed almost like an eternity for me. Today, I know that there are times that God does for us what we cannot do for ourselves. Later about 10 o'clock that night, Felipe called me from the hospital and he asked me if I was willing to pay for his cab fare if he took a taxi back home from the hospital. I told him that it was okay with me. I felt glad that he wasn't dead, and I also felt a slight level of pride for having been able to help save his life. Yet, when Felipe knocked at the door, my pride quickly turned into rage because I thought that at least he would feel grateful that I had saved his life. Instead, I found myself dealing with someone who was in complete darkness about what had happened that night. Felipe neither showed shame nor any remorse; he acted as if nothing had happened that night, and he started demanding that I give him back his drugs since he "knew" that I was already shooting them up! It seemed that just at that point when I found myself starting to argue with him, I suddenly experienced a moment of clarity, and I realized just how insidious this disease of alcoholism and addiction is. After a few more minutes in that heated discussion, I eventually got quiet and I turned around and went into my bedroom and I came back into the kitchen with his bundle of drugs that he was still demanding from me with incessant cries and screams. I didn't see Felipe again until I had about three years in recovery when I ran into him on a public bus on Bergen Avenue in New Jersey. He looked very thin and he told me that he had contracted the AIDS virus and was on that "cocktail" medication to control his symptoms. Once I had heard a statement that left a bad taste in my mouth, but if I look at it from a positive point of view, there are times when some of us have to die so that others can live. My friend Raymond who took me to that first meeting eventually died as a direct result of this disease. My other friend Miguel who was also a part of my early recovery also ended up contracting the AIDS virus, but as far as I know, he is still alive but in poor health. I could continue telling you of hundreds of other cases like these where this disease destroys on a daily basis the lives of people, their families, and entire communities. I don't know why I'm still alive, but I believe that everyone in this world has his or her purpose for being here. I no longer ask for explanations since it no longer seems important. I feel tremendously grateful with the blessings that God has granted me and I no longer complain or feel sorry for myself as I used to do in the past. I know that most of the terrible things that have happened in my life as well as those tragic events were not God's fault but of those other human beings who carried some of the same pain and suffering deep within them as I did deep within me. Today, I understand the evil that existed within Don Julio's heart when he took my mother's life. Today, I don't blame my father for having been the alcoholic that he was. I blame no one for becoming the savage that I became since I understand that Don Julio did not put those drugs and alcohol into my hand, neither was it my father who threw that garbage into my body – it was solely me and only me who made that choice and I am responsible for the damage that I brought into the lives of so many people. At the beginning of this book, I referred to myself as a person who was born sick and who spiraled down to the point of losing touch with all of those productive values that serve as a guide throughout our development. Yet I have no doubt that there were some circumstances that happened during my early development, which accelerated my disease up to the point when my life became a complete disaster. The reader might ask "How is it that I can be assured that I was born sick into this world?" This question might become a philosophical battle for every human being in this world suffers from one or another emotional or spiritual deficiency. After many years of self-examination, I have discovered a plethora of emotional deficiencies, which kept me a victim to my own destruction. By no means do I wish to present myself before the eyes of the world as someone who is better than anyone else, but I will tell you that I am the only one responsible for myself and I have no power over another living human being. It is by this principle that I try to live my daily life whereby I am responsible for the things that come out of my mouth, my behaviors, and my attitudes towards the society that surrounds me. I know quite well that it was my diseased/sick attitude and my unpleasant behavior, which created a numerous problems in my life. Today, I have a chance to look at my past and see just how unpleasant my life was and every day, I can ask myself if I would like to go back and live that way again. The answer to that is "NO". When I open up the doors to my past and I review the events of my life without spending too much time stuck in my past history, today I can see clearly what type of a person I have now become and I feel a new level of gratitude each and every day in my life. I don't feel any hatred towards anyone. I have forgiven Don Julio for having stolen the life of my loving mother Gladys on that sunny day. I don't allow resentments to crop up in my life since I know the damage that they create in the life of a sober alcoholic and addict, and I know just how emotionally sick they can make me. The resentments that I had against my Grandmother and the animosity that I felt for the lack of love and nurturing that she couldn't give me are no longer obstacles in my mental and spiritual growth. Today I understand that the same rage that I had over my mother's murder also created in my Grandmother the same inability to give to anyone her love. I believe that she did the best that she could with the little that she had to give me a roof over my head, food, and clothing, and I'm very grateful for this. I know quite well that today there is much help available for families who are going through what we went through during those years and it's possible that maybe a psychiatrist could have helped us to heal some of the emotional pain that was caused by the deaths of my mother and father. Yet with everything that happened to me and my family, that doesn't give me an escape for me to not take responsibility for the unfair/unjust acts that I committed against other people. Previously, I had started explaining about hate, resentments and rage and I mentioned about the damage that these negative emotions will cause to the spiritual and emotional growth of a human being, and I would like to say that just as these last three emotions, there are various others that also affect people on a daily basis, and the worst part of that is that we are completely oblivious about them and we sometimes don't want to admit them because we are comfortable with them despite the damage that they may cause to others. Later on in this reading, I will share with you a list of the defects of character that cause problems in a human being which I have termed "emotional sickness of the spirit" or "mental maladjustments" since they all stem from the mind of a human being. I will then describe most of the situations that create destructive/damaging thoughts which leads a person to continue living in a self-destructive manner and therefore, in constant trouble with alcohol and controlled substances and other areas of your life. There is no doubt in my mind that the worst hell is contained within our own mind, and it is in this place where most of the problems that we create for ourselves begin. Today, I am convinced that the disease of alcoholism and addition is only a symptom of a greater problem that we have created throughout our lives since we have ignored the many "signs" which have taken us to the point of physical, emotional, and spiritual destruction. However, I don't want to sound like a "know it all "or like someone who holds a doctorate in psychology, but I do wish to give the reader a chance to examine their life in order to find the reasons as to how alcohol and controlled substances have come to own their soul. During the years that I was shut away inside of that disgusting prison, I never had the chance to get to know who I was since I existed in a world where the reality of life did not exist, and I never had the good fortune to get to know myself. It would be a great shame if I were to spend the rest of my existence still lost in that mental darkness/obscurity which brought so much misery to my life and to the lives of so many other people who were not to blame for anything.

<u>Chapter IV – Mental Maladjustments</u>

Most of the facts that I'm going to provide to you have been those that I've had the privilege of learning from numerous other people who have learned them from personal experience/practice, especially those facts which have been more difficult to accept in order to be able to get them under control through pure vigilance, and others have been acquired from voluminous reading. It is these facts that are of great importance for the emotional and spiritual growth of living beings, and I will tell you that it doesn't matter what type of person one is – most people in this world are afflicted with them. In other words, once does not have to be an alcoholic or an addict in order to become the victim of these maladjustments which create such devastation in a human being and in our personal relationships with others. After many years of study about myself and my character, I can tell you that I have been able to see how these ugly traits have created so many unpleasant situations, both for myself and those people around with whom I have personal relationships, it is by self-discovery that I am freed daily from the unstable emotions and sick feelings that often I go through. And, it is in this way that I can find the daily spiritual peace that helps me to get closer to God's divine grace. I will now outline a number of these mental maladjustments and sick feelings which do not allow for spiritual growth and which keep us victims of sick behaviors in our lives. **SELFISHNESS** for me takes the lead in the parade since it is this defect that tells me that no one else is important, and that I'm first. I don't care for the rest of humanity around me and if I do help someone, I do so because way in the back of my mind, I have hidden motives to do so. Compassion does not exist for me since I'm always first and the world around me means nothing for me. What interests me is the benefit that I'm going to get out of those people around me, be it financial, sexual, or materialistic. In the end, the result is always the same – everything is based upon me. The greatest act of selfishness in a human being is the act of committing suicide, be it because you take your own life by your own hand or because you choose to take your life away little by little in the presence of those people around you who love you. The selfishness that such a person has is at the greatest level of darkness that exists since that person doesn't have the capacity to find clarity within their scattered mind, and alcohol and drugs give them the courage to go through with such a decision. The level of selfishness that existed within me was of such magnitude that I couldn't see this reality, and there were many times when I found myself "visiting" the doors of death and moment by moment, God rescued me from that place. The selfishness that existed in my life was one of great proportion and dimension that covered the greater part of the moral fiber of my being. If after reading this story any of you feels as if you have a conscience and if you examine it, you can find in it the many occasions in which you can see your own self-centeredness affecting your lives, it is then required to get out of this place and accept that you're suffering from this destructive personal spiritual sickness. Throughout the years, my level of **HONESTY** was never visible since from a very young age, I learned to lie in order to survive in the world around me. The lessons that I learned in the fields of the coffee plantation when my Uncle first slammed me against the wall dictated the beginning of my pathological lies, which later became such apart of me throughout my life. I was never one to speak the truth; I never had a sense of honor nor was I ever sincere with <u>anyone</u>. It's quite fitting that today I have to remember that the person that I need to be honest with daily is myself since I can't fool myself; the results would be disastrous for me. For example, whenever I visit a doctor, it's required that I let them know about my alcoholic condition as well as my addiction to other substances. It's my duty to protect my recovery or otherwise, any medication that might be prescribed for me could be the cause of addictive effects upon me and it may become the cause of my destruction all over again. I've seen how many people have been victims of such stupidity by lying to themselves thinking that they can take these medications and the results have been disastrous for them. Recently when I was forced to undergo back surgery, I explained to my surgeon all about my disease of alcoholism and addiction; he looked me in the eye with great surprise since there aren't too many people who can relate to this reality. After my surgery was over, it seemed that he "forgot" the conversation we had had and once I was released from the hospital, he gave me a prescription for Percaset for the pain which I later then tossed into the garbage can without giving it a second thought. Once you know yourself, and once you know your malady, it's easy to distinguish between what's right and what's wrong and thus you can protect yourself from the destruction that these substances can cause you. In the past, I would have taken those 90 Percaset in about two hours and they would have had to call the National Guard to protect the front doors of all pharmacies since my obsession for that garbage would have had serious consequences for me. Now, I'm going to mention another of these diseases that are created in the mind which affect a human being daily, and that one is called the **EGO**. This is the one that reflects the type of person that I am and everything is based on me. I'm that kid who is playing the part of the producer and the artist of the comedy. I'm the best and the greatest thing to have stepped onto the surface of the planet, and no one measures themselves against the measuring stick that I use to gauge myself since I'm better than everyone else and there is no humility in me. With this behavior, it's easy for me to judge others and to point the finger at them since I'm perfect and they're not. It's difficult to look at yourself like someone with an inflated ego since in your twisted mind, you think that you're a human legend. This person with an over-inflated ago tends to have narcissistic personality disorder with a sense of self-importance and extreme preoccupation with self. Their reactions are way out of proportion, and rage, shame, humiliation is what they concentrate on. They are good manipulators and will take advantage of other people, always bragging about themselves and their talents and achievements. They are always preoccupied with fantasies of success and are obsessive with power, good looks, or incredible stories of ideal love affairs. They do not care for other people's feelings, and they lack empathy. These individuals will pursue many selfish goals with no regard or consideration as to who they hurt in the process. This person will usually have problems with alcohol and drugs, and many failures in personal relationships, in the home structure, as well as in the community. These mentally maladjusted people usually will defend self with incredible justifications and rationalizations. This incredible malady will present itself in man and well as woman. But it is the male that will rebel against single, straight women in power.

Now in this process, we next encounter this other "rock" that can become a personal obstacle in our lives and can block our spiritual growth, and that happens to be **PRIDE**. This is something that in moderate measure is not an unpleasant characteristic, but when it gets to be out of the norm, it becomes something repulsive towards those people which whom we have constant communication with. Usually if someone doesn't know you or deals with you frequently, they can't notice this characteristic and maybe it's possible that they might eventually notice it due to the way that you behave, act and express yourself. **PRIDE, EGO,** and **GRANDIOSITY** are connected by the same thread since they're in the same family, and this combination makes me seem like a person who is superior from the rest. I'm the most intelligent, I have a high position within society, my finances, wealth and material belongings surpass yours, and my mouth is constantly full of praise for myself. Yet inside, I feel like trash/filth because my insides are not the same as my outsides, and everything I do is a front. In that same way, we come to another one of those sick obstacles that don't allow for spiritual and emotional growth since we are affected by a sickness that is created within the self, and thus, we've come to the door of **ENVY**, that two-headed monster which doesn't allow me to live a life of gratitude about the material things that I have. I'm always looking around me complaining about those things that other's have since I feel I deserve so much more than what they have. This creates within me unbalanced emotions about how I live my life and what level of gratitude I live it with. Envy covers many areas of self and the sad part about it is that we don't see it or if we do we don't addressed it because we don't know how. Once while talking to a friend, he explained to me that God has my blessings on a list and He grants them to me when He finds it convenient, and he told me that everyone else in this world has their own blessings and that they're not all the same. If you want blessings to come to your life and to the lives of your loved ones, you have to make the effort and sacrifice to get them since they're not just going to show up at your doorstep while you're sitting in the living room watching television! Yet, he also told me that the biggest blessing that any human being can have is love for his fellowman since usually love can crumble the biggest obstacles that show up in your life. Yet, I'd like to tell you that this was a quality that I had in my life, but if I did have it, it was based on the superficial things that you gave me in that moment when I got what I was looking for. It was very difficult for me to feel love for anyone when in my heart I felt nothing but **HATRED**; it consumed my daily existence since it was such a part of my life for so many years. It's difficult for clarity to enter into a dark heart, and when there is no clarity, everything around you is in complete darkness. There is no compassion, understanding, affection, respect, humility, brotherhood, nor anything else that might have to do with love. Self-pity is the owner of your existence and you live full of bitterness with everything around you since you don't love yourself. It was my experiences at a young age that dictated to the greater part of my sick growth, and my Mother's murder by Don Julio began to transform my **HATRED** into something that made me someone with a destructive heart an in complete darkness. This was one of the greatest obstacles with the most consequences to my existence, which dictated the type of live that I lived. Today, I know that forgiveness towards others is required to be able to live a life in which spiritual peace can reign within your heart. Yet another obstacle that doesn't allow you to find peace within yourself is **RESENTMENT**. Resentments towards others due to their incorrect actions don't allow me to see the clarity that enriches my heart since this is a permanent obstacle in my day and in my life, and it's usually harmful to me. When I think about something that has happened to me or some event that has happened in my life which has given me a negative feeling and I entertain that thought in my mind for a long time, once again, I start to feel rage about that incident that happened to me and while my mind is lost in that whirlwind of negative thoughts, my character/behavior usually becomes unbearable and it's unpleasant to live with me. It's important to remember that we live in an imperfect world in which human beings suffer from different spiritual illnesses and mental maladjustments, and if you can understand this concept in your mind, it's possible that you can continue to forge ahead in your life and not allow a resentment to take you outside of your spiritual growth. Is usually when acceptance takes the front seat and becomes the vehicle that takes you to that new destination where spiritual peace returns back into your day, and the hours that you wasted thinking about how you were going to get back at those who did something to you or what punishment you were going to dole out to them were wasted unnecessarily since in the end, the person who came out hurt was you. There are numerous other emotional deficiencies which cause deviations to one's spiritual growth and which keep you a victim to your own personal destruction and to the destruction of others, and another one of these is **RAGE**. Rage is a luxury that carries a damaging price for the person, their home, and personal relationships towards other people, and it's also connected to hate and resentments; they create a monster within society. Now, let's just pour some alcohol on top of these three emotional deficiencies and we'll see what happens to that person once that poison goes into their body. Rage, just like hate and resentments, are emotions which a person who abuses alcohol and other substances cannot control them since usually, they sprout out of the deepest part of yourself since you have never looked at them or you have never taken the time to correct them. Most of my life was controlled by RAGE, and my personal experiences that I witnessed allowed me to justify my acts of violence against other people without seeing my mental maladjustment. These ten basic examples make the life of an alcoholic and addict a destructive hell within their personal life and in the lives of others, and the last one of these will allow you to see how **LAZINESS** is another unpleasant attribute in our lives. It's a personal deficiency since the majority of alcoholics and addicts are ungrateful people who think that we deserve it all, and that the world owes us a living. We live under the justification that it's easier to cheat, steal, lie, and do damage in the community rather than make a few sacrifices to have the appropriate things in your life. There are alcoholics who justify their drinking because while they might have a job, they're stealing their family's sustenance with the use and abuse of these poisons, or they're stealing hours from their employer by their "lazy" excuses. They can't see that they're robbing their children and/or spouses of joyful moments, and they can't see the damage that they do since they're in complete darkness about their behaviors. Usually, the alcoholic or addict who has a job uses hundreds of lies to hide his disease and his work performance deteriorates, but they cannot see it. Most of the time, their family has to use a myriad of excuses to hide that person's disease and then the problems start emerging within the family unit until this disease starts to break down the relationships both at work and at home since we now find ourselves dealing with someone who is completely irresponsible about his/her responsibilities. I would like to tell you that I wasn't maladjusted in all of these areas that I have mentioned, and maybe you might ask yourselves who made me an authority on them; the answer to that would be many long years of personal self-examination, and I will also tell you that it has also been through working within myself and with my character that I have frequently discovered these unpleasant truths. Yet, I will tell you that in my years of self-discovery and while working with others like me, I have been able to little by little come out of that mental darkness which had me oppressed for so many years. Now, I would like to mention another group of emotional afflictions that cause us problems in our lives and in the lives of other people. As I had previously explained in this reading, alcoholism and addiction are symptoms of a personal and emotional disease that leads to spiritual decay. We already know that it's not only those people who have problems with this destructive substances who suffer from emotional disease and incorrect behaviors since throughout my years, I have had the pleasure of being able to share my life and recall mental notes on numerous cases where I have witnessed these mental maladjustments affecting the lives of so many people. One of these is called **INFERIORITY**. I can say that this afflicts many human beings in either small amounts or in many numerous forms, and this has a lot to do with how you were raised and the lack of self-esteem in your life. It also has much to do with the society in which we live and what we witness in our lives either visually or from those emotions that we have hidden within ourselves. Usually, a person who doesn't feel good about themselves will often change who they are quite frequently since he/she wishes to be accepted by others and while he/she are changing like the chameleon, they don't wish to look at themselves since inside, they don't want to accept what it is they really feel about themselves. Since I don't like who I am, which makes me feel terrible about myself, I want to be someone else. The answer to this and many more of these inferiorities is self-love. As a very young child, I remember feeling so different from other children; I didn't feel attractive or good enough so that others would like me. I never really understood this but I covered it up as best as I could since I didn't want anyone to discover my secret. I was a fraud, a lie, and an impostor. I looked like gold, but I felt gold-plated. When you feel spiritually unbalanced, and when you think about yourself as "less-than", you will continue your life feeling like less of a person, and you will never give yourself the recognition that you deserve. There were many times while in the midst of having conversations with other people, I would end up physically assaulting them because many times I thought that they were referring to me in their comments. When you feel inferior to others, when you have uncomfortable feelings about who you are, you will try and you will find the way to run from who you are since reality is a bitter pill to swallow and usually, the escape from yourself is made easier through the bottle or with controlled substances or through another avenue of personal self-destruction. It is the destructive comments that come out of the mouths of others which create unstable emotions within you, and if you allow these statements to affect the way in which you perceive who you are in this life, there is a possibility that you will live a life full of inferiorities and an unbalanced existence. For example, I can remember negative comments made by my Grandmother towards me and the damage that they caused to my self-esteem. On numerous occasions, I heard words that caused me great pain such as "You'll never amount to anything...you're worthless...you're a twisted tree just like your Father and you'll never straighten yourself out." For many years, I saw myself in that way since I didn't think that I deserved anything good in my life. Today, when I look back at my life and at all the gifts that God has granted me, I feel different about myself than I used to, and I am grateful that my God did not make a piece of junk, and that I'm not that twisted tree that I was for many years; I have straightened myself out. Today I have a different opinion about myself. It might be that these mental, emotional and spiritual maladjustments are not obstacles in your life, and it might be that once examined carefully, we might be able to find those that are creating unpleasant situations for our personal lives, and we can dedicate the necessary attention to them to correct them. However, you can also continue to ignore them, cover them, and hide them and remain sick mentally, emotionally, and spiritually. Throughout the years, I have experienced how **JEALOUSY** can destroy certain personal relationships with the opposite sex, and I have realized that the majority of my problems were based on fear, insecurities, control, and my complexes/ low self-esteem. **FEAR** plays the biggest part in the loss of romantic relationships, which then invites your mind to plant disastrous doubts in your life, and when accompanied by your insecurities and complexes/ esteem issues, allow for **CONTROL** to become a horrible monster to live with. When I have hidden doubts in my mind towards the person who you're in relationship with, when you don't really know what it is that you have next to you and you live life in a complete state of uncomfortability with yourself since you don't like yourself, **FEAR, INSECURITY, CONTROL** and **LOW SELF-ESTEEM** are to blame for the romantic problems that we get involved with. If I have a secret agenda within a hidden part of myself about what it is that I want to get from that relationship, I will usually never be satisfied because I will always have an expectation about the benefits that I'm going to get out of that relationship. Today when I look at the type of person that I have become, I give thanks to my God for allowing me the opportunity to see all of those obstacles which created those unpleasant situations in my lifetime. Today, I know that I do not own anyone, and I also know that everything in my life is temporary and if I don't pay attention, and I don't remember that those people that God puts in my life all have a purpose for being in my life and I try to instead control them, and I don't allow them to grow in their lives since my **FEAR** continues to keep me a victim of my own mental destruction, then my spirit is not aligned with God's will. **FALSE MACHISMO** is another one of these unpleasant qualities that prevent spiritual growth since it doesn't allow you to be the person that God created you to be. It's usually when my insecurities and my **FEAR** get wrapped around **CONTROL** which then starts dictating to me how I must present myself to others since I think that under my guises of "the dictator", "the tough-guy", and "the control-freak", I will let others know that they must respect me since I know what's convenient for them to do in their lives. I'm the best, the greatest thing that has come to this world, and I walk around with a degree of arrogance, which doesn't know what humility is since I feel superior to others. Nothing moves around me without my say-so since I'm king of the castle, and in this castle, things are done the way that I want since there's no room for two kings to rule. When in your twisted mind you create ideas for yourself that are outside of the norm, and you think that because you bring in the financial support to your home that this gives you the right to mistreat those people around you. This should make you see that your unacceptable behavior makes life heavy for those people whom you should give them your unconditional love and instead come down from that throne which keeps you living your life in constant battles with your unbalanced emotions. Today I keep in mind that I don't have the power to demand that anyone live their life under the rules that I dictate since I'm as small as a tiny grain of sand. I'm not that enormous/grandiose being who always wanted to look good. I also know that it was my self-will that caused most of my dilemmas since it dictated my lifestyle for a number of years. I have no control over anyone since I know that people around me are going to do things as they wish and when I get out of the way, they can learn from the headaches that they create for themselves. The only thing that I can do is live my life and try to understand who I was and who I want to be since I think maybe that will be God's will for me. It's no longer important for me to view myself through the eyes of grandiosity. The opinions of other people don't have the negative impact within me that they used to. I know that the majority of this world lives mentally and spiritually unbalanced. There are other obstacles to mental and spiritual growth which keep a human being in constant emotional pain since it does not allow for your spirit to grow with the necessary peace to be able to accept the mistakes made, and while your conscience keeps you trapped due to your destructive acts against those people that surround you, you will never have peace in your life. It is the feeling of **GUILT** that keep you feeling emotionally disgusted with yourself and it doesn't allow you to move on since it keeps you hostage to your own mental torture. When you live in a constant state of mental disturbance, it's very difficult to find peace within yourself and when you have no peace within, you live in total mental obscurity since you can't find a way out of that terrible place in which you find yourself. It's extremely important to open up the doors to your past, to look at your mistakes, to accept them and then move forward as you try to not repeat those same mistakes again. It's at this point that you have to learn to forgive yourself for what you've done since otherwise, you will continue your life in complete spiritual disarray, and your mental growth will never reach your door. When we were using alcohol and drugs, we never lived in peace with anyone since there was no peace within us, and we would create hundreds of unpleasant situations against hundreds of people, and the damage that we caused will always leave its mark. Yet, this doesn't mean that because this happened, you can't try to repair the majority of this damage and by example, lead a better life and stop being the public nuisance that we were in the past. This means that the main key is acceptance and forgiveness of yourself; this will help you to live in peace with yourself, and your spirit will begin to grow with the grace of God. Now that we've examined these examples, and if we notice that we're off balance with some of them, it's possible that we will notice which ones we will need help with, and just by seeing these within ourselves, it will gives us the needed awareness to find a solution. Yet, when we see these and we do nothing to correct them, we remain the victims of our own emotional and personal demise. We now reach the last personal block that causes so much mental confusion in a person's life. **LUST** has been designated to be responsible for destructive consequences in innumerable romantic relationships. We know well that since the beginning, God created man and then he created his female companion with the purpose that they not spend their lives alone. Throughout time, human beings have always searched for companionship, something which we completely trust in since we think this is what causes our very own existence to be more comfortable throughout our days. Yet without noticing, we let go of certain morals and basic principles in our lives since we don't care what price other people have to pay. Throughout my life, I have had the good fortune of sharing my live with those of the opposite sex and most of the time, my greatest problems were created by me due to my selfishness, my hate, my control, my jealousy, my insecurities, my dishonesty, and rage. These were the cause of my relationship failures and while I was living with these partners, I thought that it was their duty to be submissive to my carnal desires and whenever I would hit an obstacle in a relationship, I simply would let my eyes roam around in search of another one who would "understand" me since in my mind, I had hundreds of sick excuses to ensure that things would be perfect like me. Most of the time, alcohol and other substances gave me the security that I never felt since I was never pleased with what God had granted me since I always wanted everything the way that I wanted it. In a world where there is so much mental confusion and lack of spiritual growth, it's difficult to find someone who doesn't suffer from one or another emotional deficiency. an If you have someone in your life who gives you the best of themselves, why is it that you don't feel okay with what's around you? It's quite difficult to feel good with what's next to you when you don't feel good about yourself, and usually, your sexual behavior provides you with an escape so that you feel some temporary relief within yourself until the next excuse arrives, and the race/cycle starts all over again. For most of my life, I have tried to get a lasting relationship with a partner whereby we could enjoy those good things that God grants us. Yet, in the process of doing so, there are obstacles to our mental growth that affect the growth of these romances. From the beginning, it was my intention to ensure that these relationships would be productive and long-lasting, and yet, either due to the mistakes that I made or maybe due to the unpleasant defects of whatever partner I had next to me at the time, I find myself walking away and thinking that it would be better to try somewhere else. In that process, I leave behind someone who came out wounded by my unfair behavior. She lost years of her life, I lost years of my life, money was lost, resentments were created, along with bitterness towards our actions. In the end, there was yet another woman in my life who had been hurt since we never took enough time to try to repair all the things that were out of the norm. God has granted me the chance to be able to look at myself and see some things about myself which were in complete disarray, and today, I know where I have made some mistakes and why I made them. I'm satisfied with the understanding and the experiences that I've had the good fortune to experience since from every romantic experience that I've had, something good came out of it; my discoveries about myself have been of utmost importance in order for me to get to know myself, and with this, my mental and spiritual growth let's me know today where I am. If norms and correct morals don't exist, if your insecurities, the ego, your hate, your honesty, your control issues and your jealousy are not examined there's a great possibility that your romantic relationships will not be productive and enduring. Now that we've had a chance to learn some facts in this reading which once examined at length, perhaps might raise some doubts about the reasons why they keep a human being emotionally sick. And maybe if we see in ourselves a number of these facts, there is a possibility that there may be some hope to be able to live a productive life within society and within our personal relationships with others, and in this way, you can find the emotional peace that is so important for spiritual growth. The beginning of my new life came on that day when my friends Raymond and Miguel arrived to Ocean Avenue in a Toyota pickup truck, and that day was the beginning of my new existence in this world since I am certain that if that did not happened that way, today I wouldn't have the good fortune to be alive, and if I would have lived (without making changes in my life), I would have continued living a miserable existence. Today I thank God for using those two people like this to end my self-destruction and when they took me to my first 12-Step meeting, it was the beginning of a new life filled with gratitude towards my God for having rescued me from that horrific hell in which I lived for almost all of my life and where for the first time, I could see how beautiful it really is to live life. By working a 12-Step program, I've had the chance to find the courage to face every day with whatever is presented to me. Within the rooms of recovery, I have found the help that no psychiatrist could have ever offered me during all of those years when I was hospitalized in those mental wards. The amount of money that was lost seeking psychiatric treatment was replaced by putting a voluntary donation into a basket while attending 12-Step meetings and with that, I have received the best "medicine" that I have been able to grasp. When I didn't have a cent in my pocket, these people never rejected me and they never told me that I could not go in; instead, I was welcomed. Nothing has ever been demanded of me, and the solutions that people have shared with me throughout the years are still working for me which means that if something works, and you can benefit from it by simply paying attention and then putting it into practice in your life, there's a great possibility that you might once again get a little bit of common sense to realize that your thinking and your way of life never really gave you (positive) results. Therefore, why not let others help you and in that way, you can stop causing chaos in your life. It was in this place that I have had the opportunity to repair my destructive way of life and my maladjusted way of thinking. I know that I can never re-pay this debt for the education and knowledge that I have received from 12-Step programs. The very first thing that I learned was that it is the first drink or the first drug that unleashes the mental obsession and compulsion within me, and subsequently, the "monster" is let loose from it's dormant state. Alcohol was the first vehicle that took me to those destructive places in my life and once it would enter into my body, my mind would be open to any suggestion that was given to me, so I know very well that I don't have to take that first one because once I do, I'm off and running. Why should I then stop if the damage has already been done? This for me is mental clarity and spiritual growth since I'm no longer inside of that desolate dark place where I used to live my life. Now you might ask how someone who has lived in mental darkness all of their life can begin to see clarity/light in their life and find a level of spirituality? This only begins to happen when one is willing to keep their mind open and the suggestions of those people who have experienced similar situations to yours begin to make sense in your confused mind. Once you can accept and see that you never had any power over alcohol and any other substances, that's the beginning of your spiritual growth since clarity has begun to enter into your mind since you could never before accept such a concept. Once you realize this, only then can you see that you can do something each day to not pickup that poison that has brought such misery to your life and to the lives of numerous people with which you've had personal relationships. Once you identify how unmanageable your life has become, only then can you realize how destructive you've lived your life and the damage that you've done to yourself while you were lost in that disgusting self-destructive prison. There are hundreds of thousands of people who are capable of drinking alcohol since it's not a problem for them since they can have one or two and they know when enough is enough. Yet as for me, I know that one is not enough and thousands would never calm my obsession and my compulsion, and this is the difference between someone who can have a few drinks and the author who can't even have one.

The greatest gift that I have received is that my God has granted me an opportunity to find that being that was lost in that destructive cycle for most of my existence, and His other gift to me has been that of finding Ruben once again after having spent so many years in jails, psych hospitals, and at the gates of death and having been rescued from all of them. There was a section in this book in which I was explaining about pride, selfishness, ego and grandiosity, and while commenting about these monstrous realities, I will continue sharing with you how these diseased emotions create headaches in your life which then becomes in an unmanageable life for you in your obsessive mind. Thus, I'm going to outline certain diseased details within my spiritual life which are all based upon the level of honesty that today I have been able to acquire. When I comment on some of these facts from my personal life, I do so with the purpose of giving the reader some help in order to be able to fully understand the type of person that he/she is, and it doesn't mean that because I have suffered from these emotional deficiencies that the reader also suffers from them; yet, should you examine yourself deeply and you do identify some of them, what are you going to do to correct them? It's within you to find the solution. Since the time of my childhood, I remember having become a part of that lost world in which we live, and the street corners were the only home that I know, and it was on those street corners that I gave my mind the teachings and the sick habits throughout my personal growth and I programmed my mind with destructive ideas and bad habits in order to survive in that world that I lived in. After arriving into recovery and taking part in my self-examination is when I can honestly let everyone else know who Ruben really was; don't forget that I grew up out on those street corners without a constructive guide on how to live and what I learned had nothing to do with Sunday mass. Once I was on the path of mental and spiritual recovery, I discovered how I lacked the appropriate norms to live life. Yet by this time, there came to my life another tool in the person of Mrs. Carmen L and it was she who gave me the teachings and skills to begin over again with a new life. Perhaps she doesn't know how instrumental she was in my growth and I will never be able to repay her for the help that she gave me. Yet I know that she would be grateful with only knowing that my life has blossomed due to her help. When I met Dona Carmen, I had some time where my twisted and dark mind would start to see some clarity once again and my change was noticeable since the people that were in my life daily were giving me their help because if "nothing changes, nothing changes" since you'll continue being your own worst enemy. Now that Mrs. Carmen L had taking me under her wing and I was doing volunteer tasks at the P.A.C.O. community center where she worked as the coordinator, I improved and got a job as an outreach worker for them and my task was to go out and make presentations to schools, colleges, etc. on AIDS Education which at that time was destroying communities in all parts of the world and which has taken the lives of thousands of people whether transmitted through unprotected sexual contact or by the use/abuse of controlled substances and the exchange of syringes between drug addicts. While I worked, I was also able to participate in different facets of recovery from addiction and alcoholism, and as I acquired more knowledge, my pride, my ego, and my grandiosity also grew out of proportion. I thought that I was the best thing to have ever arrived at the center, and I walked around with an incredible amount of grandiosity since I was completely oblivious about this part of my personality and I didn't have an ounce of humility within me; I was mentally lost again. Once day, I got to the job, and punched in my timecard, and as I was going upstairs to my office, Dona Carmen called me over into her office to speak with me. Our conversation wasn't long, but in just a few words, she shared with me two or three realities that I wasn't too happy to hear about. She told me that I was walking on around floating on air and that I should come back down and plant my feet firmly back on the ground since I wasn't the great legend that I thought I was. I told myself, "Who the hell does this woman think that she is, and how dare she speak to me in that way? Doesn't she know who I am?" And with that thought, the resentment started festering within me which lasted quite a long time. I continued on with my duties, but now I thought that it was time to partake of an office romance with a secretary who was quite a beautiful woman. She would always reject my romantic attempts/advances which gave me even more motivation to figure out yet another way how to try to win her heart. Once again, Dona Carmen called me into her office and again in just a few words, she told me that what I was trying to do was not going to be convenient for me, and she also told me that I knew nothing about this woman and that the best thing that I could do was to give up my ideas and direct my eyes somewhere else. But just like that time when I was helping my friend to pump the gas and he told me to stick around and we ended up crashing that car at the edge of that cliff where I created yet another mess in my life and I didn't listen, in this instance, there were again disastrous consequences for me.

There is a saying that goes "In a war that's forewarned, there are no casualties." That's so true. I will tell you that there were many people who warned me that what I was planning was going to cause me grave consequence, but their words fell on deaf ears, and the price that I paid was quite high. It's a miracle that I'm still alive today. The more advances that I made to this woman, the more I was rejected. My extravagant way of dressing and the expensive jewelry that I wore painted a portrait of pure pride and grandiosity, and all so that this woman would give me the time of day and maybe spend a minute with me having a cup of coffee since I was sure that once that happened, I'd be able to get into her **bedchamber**. I remember that when I would leave work and I would get home at night, I would kneel and ask God in my prayers to help me to get the love of this woman who had created such an obsession in me. Today, I know that just because a book is beautiful on the outside, it doesn't mean that the material inside is going to be enjoyable. I also know that there are times that everyone else has more knowledge than I do, and I have to pay attention to what I'm told because in the long run, I'm the one who pays the price. I also know today that I have to be very careful about what I ask of my God since it could be that once He grants it to me, it might not be the best thing for me. That woman that I spent so much time trying to get her to notice me, that woman whom my innocent daughter told me to be careful about since she looked like a passive type – that woman later became my wife after some time, and that marriage became the worst nightmare within my early recovery. If I would have listened to Dona Carmen, my sponsor in the program, my daughter, and other people who just wanted the best for me, I would not have gone through all of the destructive and sick feelings that I suffered, and I probably could have prevented such misery in my life. Today, I have "learned to listen, and listen to learn" since it's only when I pay attention that I can put into practice the examples that others give me. Throughout my life, I have realized that the person whom I have lied to the most has been Ruben, and the lies that I have told myself have been the most detrimental to me. Therefore, I want to ask you: why is it that we lie to ourselves so often? The answer to that is because I have a mind that has been obsessive and compulsive all of my life, and it's easy for me to lie to myself since I don't have the capacity to notice it. I'll explain to you what the disease of alcoholism and addiction is all about. There were so many times where after having been incarcerated for a few years without using that poison, once I returned back into the community, I would tell myself, "You can just have one. It's not going to hurt you..." and once again, that first one would get into my system, the desire for that one would cease to exist, and once again, I was back to the races in which eventually, the law would have to intervene in my life to stop the self-destruction; this was one of those times when I had lied to myself again. Today, I know that I can't be around people who destroy themselves daily with these poisons as I need to protect what I have acquired. I also know that hanging out/ walking around with people who are still active and are suffering from the disease is not good for my mind since they are a negative magnet. On television, they present this poison as something attractive to the eyes, but they don't show you the homes destroyed, the violent deaths, the suffering of innocent children, and the deaths due to car crashes, not to mention those people that have been incarcerated for life due to the lives they took while under the violent and drunken effects of alcohol. They try to sell you a precious gift while they get rich on the misery that they dole out to the world, and the public lies to themselves with the ideas that they can control the devastation to their being. A friend of mine many years ago told me that if you hang out in a barber shop often enough, there's a big chance that in the long run, I might end up getting a haircut. In the same way, if I hang out in bars and the places where that garbage is available, there's a great chance that I might find myself in a mental place where the temptation might seem like something pleasant. In the same way that we have uncovered numerous emotional and spiritual maladjustments, I will continue to share with you about another detriment that afflicts mental and spiritual growth, **and this** one is the <u>KING/QUEEN BABY SYNDROME</u>. It affects both men and women equally since they're incapable of understanding the word "no". This tells me what I deserve, what I want to hear, and how you must look at me since I am a "King" or "Queen" and wherever I arrive, I deserve and demand the necessary attention from everyone present; in fact, they must even bow their heads when I enter into their midst. I walk with and incredible amount of arrogance and I usually have no level of humility at all – things have to be the way that I see them, and nothing that's explained to me makes any sense since my degree of arrogance is such an obstacle for my spiritual growth since I have no clarity in my brain to look at things from another perspective. I give no compassion but I want people to be compassionate with me. I just want to hear what I want to hear, and when this doesn't happen, I rebel against everyone. If things don't go the way that I want, I behave like a little Child and I scream and stomp to get my way. Most of these people don't have the skills to have constructive relationships with others and they live in personal isolation since no one understands them. Usually such a person looks for numerous excuses to keep complaining about life since he/she doesn't understand their malady and they have complaints about everything around them since they live in a state of mental darkness which they can't get out of. For most of my life, I thought that people around me were responsible for fixing my sick feelings and unbalanced emotions, and when I encountered an obstacle since these people wouldn't offer me the relief that I sought, I would usually run to find an escape and the remedy in alcohol and controlled substances; I couldn't perceive that the only person responsible of such a repair was me. Yet during this process, I would acquire resentments with these people since they didn't tell me what I wanted to hear. Throughout the years, my knowledge about my spiritual and mental recovery has been enhanced in numerous areas in which I would create numerous headaches and emotional maladjustments since I didn't want to look at the problem. and this problem was always present since the problem was me and not those people around me. It wasn't my wife or my children or the courts neither was it my family nor anything material, neither was it my friends. Everything was based on my perception of these things and with the degree of acceptance that I perceived them since I know today that the one who created that hell was me. Today there are numerous aids for people who suffer from different physical mental, emotional, and spiritual maladjustments – there are psychologists and other mental health facilities for your assistance. There are detox clinics whereby once your body has flushed itself from these poisons that we used to put into our bodies and they're no longer in your system, you can see things with more clarity. Yet this doesn't mean that just because you attend such a place to get help with this that you might get results since there are three parts that make this disease of alcoholism and addiction to controlled substances a living hell for someone. The first of these is the PHYSICAL part; once the physical body is clean of substances, if you don't attend to the mental part, usually your destructive ways of thinking tend to take you back to that same place where your mental desolation and misery were your personal companions. That's usually when a recovery program for alcoholism/addiction is most appropriate since in such a place, you will start to learn about everything that concerns this disease; once you have tended to the physical and mental aspect, bit by bit the spiritual aspect will begin to manifest since you will grasp another way of looking at life and thus your mental growth and your spirit will begin to blossom without these malevolent substances in your system.

"Happiness is the worth that you give to your life".

Chapter V – Acceptance And Recovery

Once we have acquired knowledge about this disease, and we then learn that there are three areas of great importance to our physical, mental and spiritual growth, it is only then when we can truly comprehend how destructively we have lived our lives under the influence of these **malevolent** substances. We will then also understand that acceptance is the main tool required to continue along our daily journey. Mental clarity will begin to manifest and our day becomes an amazing experience. It is very important to remember that the only way that our mental and spiritual growth will manifest within you is through self-honesty. It is then when you will frequently notice that you can keep an open mind to the suggestions that are offered or made to you in your daily life. You also need to have the ability to be willing to daily accept that **you are an alcoholic (re-phrase??) and that your life has become unmanageable in many areas since you have no power to stop ingesting these substances.** Once you can accept this, it will be the beginning of your recovery since you will now understand about the physical, mental and spiritual malady. Once you have acquired **ACCEPTANCE,** you will understand that you have also acquired a higher level of emotional maturity which had never before existed while you were involved in the use and/or abuse of these destructive substances. Once we begin to get some knowledge about this destructive **sickness/ illness** and you stop lying to yourself and once you accept your **malady within yourself,** that is when you will begin to notice that your spirit will once again come alive since you kept it dead throughout those self-destructive years. It is my daily task to keep in mind that there are hundreds of people in this world who are personally afflicted with this disease, and it is my **duty/responsibility** to bring to them some much needed help into their lives. Yet this doesn't mean that because I offer my help to those people that they will eventually see what they must see. There are times while offering people what has been freely gifted to me from the many 12-Step recovery programs available today that I have witnessed many people lose their very lives for the simple reason that they did not surrendered to the ravages of this disease while their **scattered** mind kept them lying to themselves and eventually, death arrived quite unexpectedly. I'll give you an example of this scenario which might serve as food for thought for your mind and your spirit. I consider myself a trained culinary chef and in my job, I'll prepare you a succulent dish so that it will serve your physical and spiritual sustenance. I prepare it with love and dedication after having had long hours of training in a kitchen. After creating for you such a delicious and exquisite dish, I bring it over to you where you are lost and I try to feed those areas of your life that need nutrition. Once I give you this food and I place it before your eyes on the table and you refuse to even taste it after I have explained all of its ingredients to you, you then throw it away in the garbage which tells me that what I offered you is no good and that you still prefer to follow your destructive way of life. That is when you then help me to see how your mental insanity is still keeping you a victim of your own self-destruction. I offer you what I have been given, and I do it from my heart since today I know how lost I was once on my life, but I know today that I can't force anyone and that I can't save anyone who doesn't want to be rescued. I can only try since I am not responsible for the final outcome. As I give you these basic examples on the different areas of sick growth which deteriorate you physically, mentally, and spiritually, I also want to mention another spiritual malady which is called **FEAR.** What is the reason for this, you might ask. When FAITH doesn't exist in your heart, fear in turn becomes your constant companion and it creates numerous situations in your life where you, in turn, will become a victim of your own mental and personal destruction. Once God doesn't exist in your life, and you think that you know what's convenient for you, usually your **SELF-WILL** will cause havoc in your life, and you will then see how fear will control many areas of your life. There are thousands of people who say that they know about God, but that doesn't mean that because they have heard about God that this gives them the faith to believe in this Higher Power which makes our lives something incredible to live. From my infancy, I remember rebelling against the idea that a Higher Power existed who had created me in his own image. I lived my life thinking that when something good would happen in my life, that was called "luck", and when something "bad" in my life would happen, that was just bad luck. I never thought that the good things that would happen to me where the way that my God was blessing me, and I could never see that the "bad" things that happened in my life were created by my own destructive self-will; I blamed others because it was easier not to accept my part in such destruction. There were many times in my life where fear and lack of faith caused my self-will to create unpleasant results in my daily existence. Throughout my life, I have witnessed how fear and people's personal will interfere with spiritual growth. I will give you another basic example on how an entire family will suffer the devastation that's created by one member of that family who is actively involved in the use and abuse of alcohol and other substances. Just because one member of the family is fearful about what might happen in the home once the active alcoholic is removed from the home environment, his/her own self-will keeps him/her a victim of a cycle of pure mental insanity where there is no peace in that home, and those children from that family begin to grow up with emotional diseases which in the future will cause critical problems in their personal lives since FEAR kept one or the other partners company in this tragic personal situation. Maybe one of these partners in the family is the one who brings home the financial support for that family, and the FEAR that the other partner feels does not allow him/her the ability to find an escape from this situation since he/she thinks that they will lose all of their material possessions acquired during the years of involvement in this **toxic** relationship. Yet the sick alcoholic/addict is unable to see or even determine that his/her own self-will is what's keeping him/her a victim of that fear and lack of faith. When you put your faith in that Higher Power and you stop becoming **hindrance/nuisance** within your own life, that is when you will find the freedom as to why the lack of faith, fear, and your self-will have kept you a victim of the spiritual and emotional destruction within your children and your home. Although this personal story that I have shared with you entails experiences from my life, there are hundreds of other examples that I can describe based on the knowledge of hundreds of other people who have shared their personal stories and experiences with me about the damage that the members of their families also endured. In the same way that I have cited specific examples on sick emotional and spiritual growth, I will now tell you about another one which is hardly ever seen for the simple reason that we find ourselves in complete mental darkness in terms of the self, that is **DISEASE ATTRACTING DISEASE OR SICK RELATIONSHIPS.** This happens when there are numerous similarities in the relationships that you carry with other people. This happens to me when I find myself attracted to those people because I can see in them certain behaviors that seem familiar to the sick behaviors that I see in others or in those past relationships that I have experienced before and I tend to be attracted to those relationships like a magnet since their sick behaviors allow me to feel more comfortable with myself since I can't detect a sick pattern of growth within myself. Today I realize that if I do what I did and if I practice what I used to practice, then the result will always be the same and it will result in more emotional and spiritual pain. There was a specific instance in my life where I could see this truth become a reality throughout so many years, and I witnessed the destruction that such a situation caused in various people and it left its imprint in those people who didn't have to pay such consequences. I'll give you another example so that you can see what I'm trying to explain. In my personal circle, I know a woman who chose throughout the years as her personal companions to live with four men who were all alcoholics and addicts since she was spiritually and mentally and emotional unbalanced in several areas of her life and she couldn't see it since she had no mental clarity to see these realities. After I pursued her and I eventually had a romantic relationship with her, something within me awoke and I realized that this was not what I wanted for myself, so I set my sights somewhere else, and once I targeted my sights there and I saw something/someone else who I was more attracted to, I started noticing that this new partner that I have focused on has hundreds of deplorable qualities just like the woman or men before her or him, and now it's time to find another place since I now realize that I have created a pattern in my life and I seem to keep attracting sick relationships into my life with great ease. Let's say that I continue doing this three or four more times and each woman has children in her life to raise. Do you think that those children will grow up with healthy minds after having lived in a nucleus of pure emotional sickness, pure mental and emotional **extremes?** No, I don't believe that this would happen since part of the destruction that was created effected their lives in one way or another. It has been explained to me that insanity is doing the same thing repeatedly and expecting to receive different results and today I know that reality very well. Maybe I can justify my mistakes and I can lie to myself by telling myself, "No way!! I was a good father! No way!! I was a good provider! No way!! I tried to give them love!" Yet, in the end, was I really all of those things or was I negligent with the examples that I mentioned? There is a big possibility that I will lie to myself since my sick personality does not allow me to see such a reality. God has given me the opportunity to examine myself and acknowledge a great deal of the emotional deficiencies and mental maladjustments which I suffered daily and today I do realize the larger part of these maladjustments. I know quite well that as an alcoholic and an addict, my false pride, my grandiosity, my ego, and the charismatic way in which I introduced/ presented myself to other people was what constantly helped me to get destructive relationships since I lacked the ability to see this. Today, I can see how these co-dependent relationships have numerous deplorable qualities, and these sick traits are transmitted from one person to another within the family nucleus. It's is very difficult to be able to notice such a level of darkness when your growth has been compromised with actions, ideas, and destructive values, and your self-esteem has been replaced with false pride and various other mental maladjustments in the home. These people tend to value their intimate relationships with destructive behaviors in the home, and the consequences tend to create harm be it in large or small quantities. It's very difficult to witness such a thing when you have programmed yourself with negative attitudes and values of small stature, yet these tend to appear normal in such homes. Throughout my years of personal destruction, I always saw my life as a constant problem and everything in it was a problem. Today, I see everything in my life as situations, and each situation has a solution. Only I can make my life a problem since all I would have to do is simply pick up a beer in my hand and all of those destructive thoughts would come back into my mind. Personal justification is a very destructive tool for someone since it keeps you in complete darkness with regards to your actions and keeps you lying to yourself about numerous situations in your life. Today I keep in mind that most of the world has sick skeletons in their closet, and it's my job to get rid of mine since only you know yours and they are the ones that keep you a victim of your own mental destruction. I know that when they are not dealt with appropriately, they will come out of obscurity to create emotional pain in your present and you will never find any peace in your life. Today I now carry a very different belief in my life about my sick development which is very different from the one that I used to have. This belief that I have today might be valid and it's the one that makes the most sense to me and which brings me a more comfortable degree of acceptance to my life. If we have knowledge about diseases that are passed on through inherited family genes, it's quite possible that you might understand my opinion, and this may offer you a level of relief to your being. Throughout the years, scientists have been able to determine how numerous illnesses are transmitted from one family member to another, and how in some cases, they skip from one generation to another. Therefore, is it possible that alcoholism can be inherited? As I explained to you before, this is strictly my opinion since I don't have a doctorate degree in medicine, but it is the one that makes the most sense to me, i.e. HEREDITARY DISEASES. I will now give you some examples of some other diseases passed on through the family tree, and I will try to explain why my opinion is so strong on this subject area. It has been proven that there are numerous diseases that are passed on through families while others skip through a generation and they manifest much later. If we examine this concept with an open mind and try to understand it, this may bring you some sense of relief. We know that there are various types of cancer that are hereditary; we also know that there are numerous mental illnesses that are genetically inherited, and we are also aware that diabetes is also transmitted genetically, in that same way many forms of heart disease come to the picture so why not alcoholism? It's my opinion that this and the other opinions given about these other illnesses will be the main key to find the reason – if I was born sick due to defective genes, would this be the reason why I'm allergic to alcohol and if that is the reason, what am I going to do to resolve this problem? Throughout the few 24 hours that I spend in recovery, I have learned to keep my alcoholism arrested daily by taking certain precautions so that I don't allow this disease to spiral out of control, and that is the same thing that I do with my diabetes by checking myself physically to make sure that my blood sugar is under control so that I don's suffer the symptoms that come along with this disease. I try to eat healthy, keep my weight down and I exercise so in that way, I take care of my health properly and I don't suffer any symptoms. It is in that same way, I keep my disease of alcoholism under control day by day, I keep in mind that if I also tend to it properly, my days become productive and beneficial since I have stopped lying to myself. Throughout my physical, mental, and spiritual recovery, I can honestly tell you that I am immensely grateful to know that I am and alcoholic, and maybe you are thinking, how can someone feel grateful to have this disease? I will say that it's better to know what is happening to me than to live a life lost in darkness. I know today that it's very important to address these three parts of my disease of alcoholism – physical, mental and spiritual since I know that when these parts are not in order I will usually find myself unbalanced in some area of my life, and I can see it. The principles found in various 12 Step programs have given me numerous tools to be able to keep these areas under control. It has been explained to me the things that I have to do to live a productive life far removed from my personal destruction, and I will mention that if I don't do what is suggested to me, I have realized that the one who pays the price is me. Today, I am aware how head-strong I am, and I know that my sick attitude kept me in constant problems in my past and I am aware that whatever I'm told is said to me with the purpose of giving me the help that I need. In the 19 years since I entered the rooms of recovery until today, it has worked for me. I would like to take credit for my recovery and would like to let you know that I am responsible for getting the knowledge that I have received, yet that is not proper since what this programs of recovery has given me would take me a complete eternity to repay. When I entered into this recovery process, my physical state was quite deteriorated from the use and abuse of numerous chemical substances, and my mental state was in the most disastrous shape that you could imagine, and let's not forget my spiritual state. Just like talented architects, the people in these programs began an amazing construction task combined with much love and understanding which has been incredible coupled with enormous patience and tolerance without caring about my color, race, creed, or background. They spent their time addressing my disease and little by little, day by day they made my mental growth something worthy to be appreciated. They never once told me that "You can't come in here" or "You're no good" or "You're Puerto Rican and we don't accept your kind here…" These people who in my past I would never have dealt with they were the ones who completely reconstructed my life entirely, and the level of gratitude that I feel in my heart is amazing. These people today exist in the whole world an they offer that same help to numerous alcoholics daily, and I can truly say that this works because if it worked for this twisted tree, it will work for anyone who really has a sincere desire to stop drinking alcohol. Once I was asked why this works and I will tell you that it only works when you're open minded, willing an honest with yourself this is the only way that it works, and when you accept and practice what is offered to you daily and when you put into practice the suggestions that are given to you to work in your life. This has been the only way that it has worked in my daily life. I remember in my past when my Grandmother would tell me, " Why is it that what ever I tell you goes in one ear and out the other?" I would like to tell you that wasn't like that and that I listened to everything that I had heard, but that would be a lie. Yet today when someone tells me something that makes since, I pay attention to it and I try to put it into practice because when I don't listen to what I'm told, usually later on I will regret it when I realize my mistake. However, I don't feel like I'm better than anyone else, and I don't walk around the planet like I know everything there is to know since sometimes, I can learn something from the person who has just a few hours of being in recovery, and in this way, I can learn from both women and men who are afflicted with this disease. I don't consider myself the "know-it-all" that I thought I was; I'm not that dictionary and seven encyclopedias that I thought I was since the program of recovery brought me back to reality, and that is that I am an alcoholic and that this disease is with me for life and it will blossom within me just like a bad weed if I don't tend to it properly. It's very important that in my daily life I remember that God has a purpose for my life, and I remember quite well that plea that I made to him in that dark hallway when my life was lost in darkness, and it's equally important to keep God in my life on a daily basis since he brought me into the doors of recovery and freed me from my destructive and constant obsession. It is my purpose to offer you several tools for your physical, mental, and spiritual growth, and it is not my wish to control your lives in any way with this story. My main reason and primary objective is to give you a certain amount of knowledge in some areas that might be unbalanced in your life. I will try to do so by using the mental tool of PERSONAL IDENTIFICATION. This is a tool that we can use to look at similarities within our lives and to find a way to understand this things and/or occurrences in our lives. If you use this tool as a means to compare, you will never be able to see how disastrous your mental condition is. Yet if you use it like a positive object in your life, I will tell you that there is no doubt in my mind that you will see the numerous areas in which you have experienced numerous similarities within your own personal destruction. For an alcoholic, it's not a requirement to visit a jail, or to lose his/her job, or that his spouse has him arrested for his abusive behaviors in the home. It's also not required that you witness painful situations in your life or that you visit psychiatric hospitals in order to become an alcoholic. If once you take a drink of alcohol into your hands and you cannot stop drinking, that is a sign that you're suffering from this disease. If you try to control your use and every time you drink, it becomes out of control, that's another sign. If you tell yourself, "I'm just going to drink this weekend because I worked hard all week," that is yet another reason since your looking for reasons and excuses to justify your next drinking binge. If after taking several or numerous drinks you don't remember what you talked about with other people, and you feel uncomfortable with yourself because you don't know whom you might have verbally offended, that's another example. If your personality changes and you become someone else who behaves aggressively, is violent, or offensive with other people, these also are signs of pure insanity once your drinking gets out of control. If you drink because you don't know how to mingle in social situations with others, and once you put that poison into your system, you become someone else that you don't even recognize, then you've arrived at the gate of PERSONAL IDENTIFICATION. Yet in the same way, there are hundreds of other similarities which are symptoms of alcoholism. One of these is personal desperation and obsessive thinking with regards to alcohol. If you can't forget your past, and you're in constant pain in your present, and the only way that you find relief is through drinking, that is yet another sign that there is no serenity in your being and no peace, you have once again identified. If you constantly feel sorry for yourself and you feel worthless to the world, you have found yet another reason to identify. However, if your self-centeredness starts to disappear and other people begin to matter in your life, you might be able to notice that clarity is starting to develop within your shattered person. Today, I can identify with hundreds of people daily, and I stopped saying, "I never did that" or "I wasn't like that" in order to keep finding excuses in my life. If you can then notice that while alcohol is not in your system, you can function without it and you don't feel those painful feelings that you felt, and you no longer smash the entire set of dishes, and car accidents no longer happen to you, and you don't end up in a jail cell as you did in the past, and you have loving and productive relationships in your home and in the community, and you no longer lose jobs, maybe you will be able to realize that it's better to live your life without this destructive poison. My purpose with this reading is to highlight the surface of a sick development within ourselves, and all of the examples just given take us to that same desolate place where alcohol and other substances give us a temporary escape so that in this way we don't have to look at ourselves and continue living life on that merry go round of self destruction. For many years, I sought relief for my mental, emotional and spiritual pain in so many places, and did this in order to get some relief to my sick self and my spirit which was dying due to my personal path of destruction while also in the process of destroying the lives of others. Yet, it didn't matter what I had since my soul felt an incredible desolation. Therefore, now I'm going to talk about MATERIAL POSSESSIONS. These belongings and other material objects don't dictate the type of person that I am, and although I think that my "treasures" are in great proportion, and although I might think that other people admire me because of my possessions, that doesn't mean that my spirit feels pleased within me since I'm not happy with myself. In order to feel content with myself I have to look at the world with love because if I don't love myself, how am I going to look at the world with love, and if I don't feel love for the world, there's a possibility that I will look at myself like my own worst enemy. Throughout my life, while searching for acceptance and praise, pretending to be someone else, I wanted to fulfill areas of my life which lacked personal love and I tried quite often to conquer barriers in order to feel good about myself and so that other people would approve of me. Yet after much personal examination, I have reached the conclusion that by having an attractive woman at my side doesn't make/define Ruben and by owning a luxury car, that doesn't make Ruben; while I might have extravagant possessions, these things don't dictate the type of person that I am. What's the point of having material things yet living a life of constant spiritual disturbance? None of these things give me the ability to get the needed freedom to live a life of gratitude since my spirit lives in desolation. If I didn't have an attractive female companion, or a mansion, or a great car, or money in the bank, those aren't reasons to continue my personal destruction; in other words, to live a happy and productive live, the person that I need to be satisfied with is myself, and if I'm not satisfied with myself, and I don't feel satisfied with what God has given me it's quite possible that my destructive way of being will look for inappropriate escapes to find that temporary relief that I don't have since my spirit has no peace in order to live a life of gratitude with my God. A human being has certain needs that require the necessary attention to live a fairly comfortable life such as food, shelter, heat, clothing and various other things. Yet this doesn't mean that these things aren't necessary to try to live a life under a certain amount of comfort yet while having these things you're never satisfied, there's a real possibility that your disoriented way of looking at life doesn't allow you to look and examine yourself, and you will continue seeking escape in the bottle or in other garbage. I've had the good fortune of knowing many people who have hundreds of belongings and they walk around the world as if they're better than everyone else yet they're the most selfish, lying, thieves that you can ever encounter and they never have been able to find peace for their spirit and they live miserable lives full of hundreds of mental and emotional instabilities since they have never felt pleased with themselves and these types of people are the most unhappiest types that you can know. Next, I would like to discuss that personal affliction which is called OBSESSION AND MENTAL COMPULSION which controls the greater part of the sick mind of an alcoholic or an addict.

Throughout my life I have seen how on so many occasions this destructive behavior has crept into my life to create painful situations for myself and others, and today I can say that once I examined this trait, I have acquired an ability to keep it under control. There have been many times when a simple negative word spoken to me has created numerous destructive mental dilemmas for me because I have gone on to obsess about that word/phrase for days and hours, and that word, action, or behavior by someone else has built a mental imbalance which in many occasions caused grave/serious consequences for me and others. The same thing has happened with personal romantic relationships, material possessions, and various other areas of my existence. Once my mind takes over the controls and this vehicle starts to move at top speed, it's very difficult to reduce the speed and start following certain norms of thought since I've now unleashed a monster back into society. This was the way that I lived my life while I was involved in active alcoholism and other garbage, and I would like to tell you that It only covered those two areas, but that's not the case. I will offer you a few examples of obsessions and compulsions. After spending a long day at work where you encountered certain stressors, you then get home and instead of your wife greeting you at the door with a warm welcome, she instead meets you with a certain amount of anger which then causes an uncomfortable reaction within you since you were already feeling bothered since you left work. Next, as you sit down at the dinner table to try to enjoy a meal, now comes the rest of the story. "Listen, Ruben, I have to tell you something that happened today to Ruben, Jr. at school. He had a problem with another student at school and he hit the other kid, Tony in the head and almost cracked his skull open. The school principal called me, and this is not a good situation since Tony's parents have called the police and an attorney, and now we have to show up in court since they're suing us for medical expenses and damages." Now, here's the point to all of this. Ruben, who is now mentally affected due to the previous stressors of his work day and his wife's angry demeanor when he arrived at home, begins to start feeling rage in his mind that will set off the mental destruction that will bring disastrous consequences to the home and to himself. The more that he listens to the problem, the more anger and rage he begins to feel and his level of mental sanity and his level of spiritual peace has now been affected by numerous factors – the job, his wife, Ruben, Jr., the victim Tony, the court, the attorneys and finally, the lawsuit that he now has on his hands. He now has to get an attorney, and before all of this happened, their financial situation wasn't the greatest. The more Ruben thinks about all of this, the more his rage and obsession about this whole situation increases. In his mind, he has now created hundreds of obstacles which do not allow his spirit to get a certain amount of peace so that he can take a step back and reflect properly. While he "relaxes" in his recliner, he can feel his blood boiling, and his compulsive and disoriented thoughts start to derail little by little. With one leap, Ruben jumps out of the recliner and in two steps, he barges into Ruben, Jr's. bedroom and unleashes a handful of blows on his son and thus discharging his pent-up rage from the previous events of the day – his wife's angry tone, the stresses on the job, the financial problems, the attorneys, the court date – upon his son without being able to recognize how all of this started in his compulsive and obsessive mind, and that the more mental energy he focused on all of these events, the more momentum and speed his mental compulsion gained. This pattern also occurs with jealousy, insecurities, alcohol consumption, drug use, women, material possessions and hundreds of other things in the life of a human being. Once you begin to obsess about something, your compulsive state doesn't allow you to see any clarity in order to be able to put the brakes on your derailed way of thinking. Once we make a few mental notes about all of these mental messes, we now find ourselves visiting with our friend known as THE INVISIBLE

LINE. It exists in the life of a person who drinks alcoholic beverages or uses other substances. That invisible line cannot be seen since we don't know it exists yet once it is crossed, it will uncover the progression of the disease of alcoholism/addiction within the alcoholic and/or drug user. Crossing that line no longer allows us to drink socially, and once that happens, our alcoholism starts to grow since the obsession and compulsion takes control of the person. In my years of recovery, I have had the good fortune of listening to thousands of people talk about this invisible line and explain how they were never able to realize that they had crossed over to that other place where they had become alcoholics. In my personal life, I never remember having crossed that line from my beginnings with alcohol, I drank solely for effect; in other words, quickly so that I would get lost in that darkness that would kill the pain that I carried so deep within me. Yet I know of numerous people whose intentions were to find some happiness and enjoy their days in social company and they never thought that this monster called obsession and compulsion would come to visit the doors of their lives so quickly. Yet once they realized that they had crossed that line, it was very difficult for them to put an end to it, and this only happened once they entered the doors of recovery.

Once that invisible line is crossed and you go from being a social drinker to drinking alcoholically is when you usually find yourself in that dark, miserable place from which it's difficult to see reality since you're lost in a web of personal lies, and it's very difficult for you to accept that the consumption of this poison controls your very existence. Throughout this journey that I'm on today, I have had the opportunity to gain a good deal of knowledge regarding SPIRITUALITY meaning that if we talk with thousands of people in this world, they will all offer you a different version of this incredible power – a power that was given to me from the beginnings of my existence which is perfected by my God every day. That Higher Power (which for me is a more comfortable term) is called God and it is the ultimate authority in terms of what spirit refers to and it is made up of amazing educational examples with which I enrich my heart with daily. My spirit is made up of beautiful colors, lush and abundant trees and awesome nature scenes. It has oceans and rivers which no human being can duplicate or take credit for their creation. It has thousands and thousands of animal species of diverse colors, shapes and sizes. There are depths in the oceans which cannot be visited by human beings along with an infinite universe. Imagine how much God enjoyed creating the varied fish of the Oceans with their distinct colors and shapes, and after doing all of this hard and complicated work, a human being loses the ability to look and appreciate all of this creation with reverence. Myself, along with hundreds of other people lost in the personal destruction of their lives, could never appreciate such things. This Higher Power created us in his image and he gifted us with a spirit just like his so that we could enjoy all of this beauty that has been offered to us. Throughout many years and in my scattered mind, my God-given spirit was killed bit by bit through the most unpleasant perversities ever imaginable that this world has manifested. It was under my own personal demise that slowly made my spirit non-existent since I almost extinguished it through my destructive behaviors. After having visited the deepest abyss of hell and having my spirit almost succumb under my own self destruction, my God found the way to rescue me from that terrible being that I had become, and he granted me new sight to my eyes so that I could see reality. Today I can see the destruction that was created within myself and others in this world. I keep in mind that in the same way that the good exists, in that very same way the bad also exists; there are two forces of utmost power, but one is stronger and more powerful than the other, and with that one I feel more comfortable. At one time in my life, I was an atheist who completely refused the idea that there existed a higher spirit Which is compassionate and loving and who had a purpose for me in this life. I remember that in my spiritual loss, I used to say to it that I didn't ask to be born into this world, so therefore, it's your fault that I am the way that I am. Yet today when I get up and give him my plea, usually my days are full of happiness and joy since he granted me the freedom from that horrific prison in which I lived, and he has granted me a faith to my heart that never before existed. It was my obstacles and acquired sufferings that have brought me to the place where I am today, and I live grateful for the gifts that have been offered to me since I don't want to lose this blessing that has been given to me in order to return back to that hell that my Self will took me to. All human beings have incredible blessings in our lives. We all have gifts and we are creative people with numerous abilities of mental growth, and I have realized little by little that this is where I find myself today. There are hundreds of people who have the talent for painting a scene with and excellent touch of precision, and there are other people who are attracted to that marvelous artistic creation, and the spirit of the artist, along with the spirit of person who feels mesmerized by the artists painting, are united as one by such a beautiful creation. In that very same way, there are musicians who compose symphonies that bring great satisfaction to the ear of a person, and these people are united by this incredible creation which connects them with a great degree of mutual spiritual satisfaction. In the same way that I present these examples, the alcoholic seeks to join his spirit with those people who like himself have something in common with others, and it is under this personal union that his spirit begins to blossom with much help and the unconditional love that exists in those places; everything in this existence is joined by a higher force. Human beings would like to take credit for this but it is impossible to want to have so much power. The spirit within the human being is the perfect machinery that transports you to great places of triumph. It is the food that nurtures you and gives strength to your being to continue with your existence and wants to improve your way of being. It is the spirit that connects you to another human being during a hug, a smile, a compassionate word, or a gesture of positive affirmation, It is the spirit that makes you live your life with great joy and happiness, and if it is being assassinated on a daily basis, it doesn't have the ability to grow since you're destroying it daily with the garbage that you're putting inside of your body and it doesn't have the ability to rejoice with the good things of life. I can speak and talk about this incredible power that cannot be seen yet which is the force that guides us in our lives, and I will also tell you that this invisible power is like a river of crystalline water which once your self-will turns it into a turbulent wave, it stops manifesting the calm beauty that it used to have because you disrupted it's very existence. My basic concept of living a productive life today is my spiritual growth since this makes my connection to my God break down each difficult obstacle that is presented to me since my faith demands that I do not give up. Yet there have existed situations in my life in which I have noticed that throughout the course of my spiritual growth, I have felt the pressures of negative forces rear their ugly heads to interrupt my journey. It has been in those moments in which I have witnessed when my God has picked me up and carried me and placed me in a different place where those pressures stopped from existing and my journey has continued in the right direction. Throughout the development of my spiritual growth, I have been able to realize how on many occasions my spirit hesitates as soon as I have the opportunity of experiencing these destructive forces in our world trying to take me outside of a constructive way of thinking, and it is in those moments when I can realize how powerful that negative force is which exists around us constantly. It's my faith in God which enhances my spirit daily and which enriches my mind and my soul and   lets me know of the required action that I must take to once again continue on my journey without obstacles along my path. I would like to tell you that in the process of doing this, I haven't made any mistakes and that I have done things to perfection, yet this would be a lie but I will tell you that in other occasions when I was so lost in that garbage dumster of personal destruction, the actions that I would have perhaps taken would have caused disastrous results for my existence. I have had the opportunity to look at my life as I have to look at it and be able to realize daily that this world around me is a giant garbage can and my job is to try to keep my area clean and while in the process be able to help those who want to clean their part since I know the joy that such a thing gives me to see another person come out of such personal destruction. It would be very easy for me to say "Your problem is not my problem", yet that would be a lie since I know very well what it is to be lost and what it is to feel the freedom that my imprisoned soul felt in this world. My God has given me the ability to open my eyes which had a destructive blindfold, and I can see every day how a human being can destroy his spirit, and in thousands of cases, death arrives sooner than what they imagined. These opinions and examples presented are a part of the physical, mental and spiritual growth and they are only facts in numerous areas of progress   in the process of a person's recovery and spiritual enhancement since the spirit is something infinite which has no limit. In the course of this journey, my spirit has been doted with clarity which had never existed in my life since this had almost been extinguished due to my own destructive self-will and it took hundreds of experiences so that my God would grant me the ability to be able to witness such devastation to my being. I could talk about spiritual growth for numerous hours, but the word that describes spiritual growth most is LOVE since a person who doesn't feel love in their heart lives in complete spiritual darkness. In my past, it was easy for me to repeat that word like a parrot since I had heard it thousands of times and it was ingrained in my mind like a tool for personal acquisitions. Yet, how was I to feel love when I was miserable with my existence and everything that I saw left a bitter taste in my being. If we have had the opportunity to examine this reading and be able to see in it the various areas that might require some personal attention, we might be able to find enough capacity to dedicate the required time to do this and to once again begin to live life without having to destroy ourselves on a daily basis so that we can grow in different areas from our shattered spirit and our irrational ways of thinking and seeing life. There aren't enough excuses to deny yourself the ability to grow physically, mentally, spiritualy and when you deny yourself from seeing reality, you remain a victim to your own personal destruction and in the process the destruction of other people as well. One must build a FOUNDATION FOR RECOVERY, and this can only happen when spiritual clarity sparks within you. If after several years of personal destruction you realize exactly where your problem is affecting you, and once this is witnessed by you, that is then the beginning of your personal recovery. Once we accept where the derailment is, then we can begin to rebuild our destructive way of thinking and behaving and start living our lives in a positive way, little by little we will experience improvement in our lives. The first thing that I need to look at is what areas of my life did alcohol and other chemicals create or created constant problems in my life, and in my relationships with other people, be in my marriage, on the job, in romantic relationships, and hundreds of other areas within my world. Once this is accomplished and I can realize the physical, mental and spiritual maladjustments that exist, that is the beginning of a spiritual journey which has no end if you so wish. This doesn't mean that because you're no longer using alcohol or other garbage that life is not going to present you with obstacles and keep you a victim to your personal excuses, and it doesn't mean that because you no longer ingest these poisons that everything around you is now going to be perfect. What this means is that you will find another way of looking at these situations without making them into bigger problems than they need to be. It's up to you to see them as situations that can be repaired without having to run from life and face them with courage. There are Twelve Steps of recovery which are a crucial guide for my life and in the lives of hundreds of thousand of others who have found recovery. They are many other 12-Step programs and various other personal help programs for the individual that have been instrumental in my life and which have been a signpost of mental, physical, and spiritual recovery for thousands of people who wish to recover from this destructive illnesses. Now that you have realized that you have no power to control putting these poisons in your body and now that you can see that your life in unmanageable and you accept this, that is the beginning of your personal freedom since you have now arrived at the door of ACCEPTANCE. Yet once you have accepted this truth and you realize the insanity that you have in your life, then it's required for you to look above and ask from your heart to that Higher Power that he restore you to a healthier mental state, and once this happens, you will begin to notice a certain amount of clarity in your mind. After noticing some progress in your way of thinking, now it's appropriate to place your self-will, which has been the cause of your destructive derailments, into God's hands so that you can get out of the way of your worst enemy which happens to be YOU and to allow GOD to guide you forward on your personal journey. Once these things are achieved, you now begin to perceive things differently and you will realize that all of that garbage that you have locked within your scattered mind keeps you a victim of negative ideas within your life and you will then see how your conscience doesn't allow you to have peace in your life since all of your secrets keep you uncomfortable with your self and you have no peace since your constantly blocking yourself off with your sick attitudes and you can find no relief within yourself. It is then when it's important to do an inventory of your personal life be it with someone from the religious sector or with a recovery sponsor with whom you have an honest and sincere relationship and in this way, you will realize that once you clean out your "mental" house, you will feel that heavy weight lift from your shoulders and your relief will be permanent. Yet when we keep all of these secrets within your being, you will feel your personal sickness beat you daily in your life and you will never experience any peace in your soul. Now that you have done an inventory of your life and you have "cleaned house" of such secrets, it's now appropriate to admit before God, another person and yourself the damage done throughout your personal years of destruction as well as the destruction   caused to others. After this is done, that is when we usually ask God to help remove these character defects which I term "mental maladjustments" since only you can change them on a daily basis until this becomes a constant task since you can still see them within yourself. Even though God knows about them, if you don't see them, you will continue living your life being selfish, self-centered, egotistical jealous, insecure, prideful, having an over inflated ego full of rage hate, along with many other self-esteem problems and they will hinder your spiritual growth. Now, let's remember that while we were drinking alcohol and using other substances, we had innumerable failures in our lives so it's fitting that we now ask God to remove all of those obstacles that caused us constant failures in order to be able to forge ahead with his divine grace. Now that we have arrived at this place, it's appropriate to try and make a list of the people whom we have caused problems in their lives so that later on we know how to correct these mistakes that we made. I realize that most of the damage that I did was against myself, and the other harm that I caused was in the area of my family nucleus and the other one was against the entire world that surrounded me. Yet I also realize that some of that damage cannot ever be repaired, but some of it can. I also need to remember that there are many people who don't have the capacity to forgive since they also suffer from their own emotional dilemmas and spiritual maladjustments. After having made such a list, you now have to make a decision as to which of those people you will honestly approach to ask for forgiveness, and to whom you will need to repay for the harms done, be it financially or verbally by your admission of your mistakes to them. Yet, you must realize that there is the possibility that your apologies may cause new problems and that by doing so, you might re-open some old emotional wounds that may have already healed but might create yet another mess in your life. You also must be careful if by making these admissions it may create dangerous situations for both yourself and with others, it's probably best to forget the idea of an apology and simply stay away from those people since you must protect yourself. In my case, there are several people who it's convenient for me to stay very distant from them since it could cost me a very high price in my life today. Now that we've reached this point in our recovering life, it's suggested to keep a daily inventory of your attitudes and your behaviors and it's appropriate that when you make a mistake, you simply accept it and don't look for excuses to rationalize your unpleasant and offensive behavior since otherwise, nothing truly has changed about you and you will continue being the same way that you were before. Once you have been able to have some progress in these sick areas, it's beneficial to keep your spiritual contact with your Higher Power as often as possible and by daily prayer and meditation, you will get closer to his divine grace. Once we have arrived to this place in our spiritual enhancement under the personal practice of this 12 Steps, then it is your job to offer this message of recovery to others that are suffering from this terrible malady and to continue practicing the principals of this recovery program in your personal life daily. You have to remember that the only way that your spiritual growth will reach you is to free yourself and by offering your help to those less fortunate ones than you. I had mentioned earlier that part of my knowledge has been acquired from other people, and part of my growth I've acquired through doing lots of reading and another part from personal practice; most of the examples given are those that I practice in my daily life since once I am aware of my personal deficiencies, it's easier for me to accept such responsibility to keep myself mentally and spiritually fit in order to live in an appropriate manner. Everything that I have done with this writing is to try to open the channels of mental and spiritual growth, and realize that if you want to live your life in unity and spiritual growth, there are hundreds of books out there available for your personal help which provide a deeper understanding of certain spiritual teachings in greater detail. There are the 12 Steps and 12 Traditions found in all of the known 12 Step programs which are a guide of concrete information which you can review and study in depth to assist you in your process. There are numerous books on recovery available for your spiritual growth if you accept your alcoholism and/or any other addiction that you might have which is currently an obstacle in your life and in the lives of others. Admitting the problem is the key, and keeping an open mind is the solution for your personal suffering. Now, it's up to you to accept it. The First Step in any 12 Step program is the only step that must be done to perfection on a daily basis since you must realize that you have no human power over any of these poisonous substances and you must accept that your life has become unmanageable and as you accept these concepts daily, you will see and feel the difference once you stop using excuses to keep ingesting these poisons into your body. Once you place this step into daily practice, you will see how you will then continue to practice the other 11 Steps in your life more frequently. This story contained in these pages was not told with the purpose of looking at myself as someone who has tons of knowledge about life. Nor have I done so to see myself as someone who is gifted with a vast cultural knowledge or with long academic titles and degrees. It hasn't been written to present myself as someone who is fearless or brave since there is no doubt that as far as alcoholism is concerned it does not discriminate, this story has simply been written with the purpose of opening doors which have been shut by someone in whom mental darkness is plainly evident and permanent in various areas of their life. Yet, maybe you can't find the appropriate clarity to start living your life in a more productive way without personal escapes or excuses. It is my purpose throughout these pages to let the reader know that there is another way to live and it is within you to find it or otherwise, you can continue living the way that you're living, and the result will always be the same – the same emotional and spiritual bankruptcy. I would love to present myself before you as someone who is perfect and who doesn't make mistakes. I would love to say that my life doesn't offer me financial situations, or health problems, and that I'm a specimen of pure mental health, and that everything in my life is perfect. Yet, this would be a lie since I still have many responsibilities which I have to handle daily in order to live a productive life. The first one of these responsibilities is to remember that I have a disease that doesn't sleep and must be treated on a daily basis; otherwise, there is a possibility that my past will become my future in a second, and that is why I am vigilant every day where this malady is concerned. I find myself extremely grateful to know that I suffer from this disease of alcoholism since I now have stopped living in that darkness that I used to live in and I can give it much needed attention so I can keep it arrested every day as I do with my diabetes. There might be many people who will read this story who might ask themselves how can a human being can mentally crash to such a point and the answer to that question is through spiritual weakness. If during the course of my existence on this earth I killed my spirit and my maladjusted mind for 25 or 30 years, how is it possible to find improvement for myself in only a few months? It would be impossible to repair something that you constantly and frequently destroyed for so many years. Yet I will tell you honestly that the person that I was had to die so that the "new" me could be re-born, and that re-birth happened on the day that I accepted that I was my own greatest problem, and when I put those poisons far away from my reach. When I arrived at the doors of recovery on the 2nd of November of 1990 at the age of 36, I never could have imagined what my God had in store for me, and if someone at that time had told me what was going to come into my life, I would have told them that they were crazy since my maladjusted mind had never experienced so many glorious blessings since it was in complete darkness. After having slept on the carousel in that little park on Bartholdi Avenue for a few days, knowing what it was like to be hopeless, helpless, downtrodden, hungry and homeless while having reached a bottomless pit of darkness, our God saw fit to begin allowing some clarity to enter my spirit and my shattered mind and slowly with the help of other recovering people, my life began to flourish. There are times that although you can't see the progress in you, other people can see the change within you. One early morning after having some time in recovery on an a particular day around 5 a.m. when my mind was clear and my thoughts flowed like clear crystal water while I was sitting at my kitchen table composing a piece of music, I remember having told my God who had never before existed in my life in prayer, "Lord, how I would like for this song to be heard on the radio. Please grant me the ability to do this." Once again, my God heard my prayer and he granted my wish just as he did that time in the dark hallway of that prison when I asked him to help me since I no longer wanted to live in darkness. A few weeks later while I was attending one of my son's baseball matches, God put in my path the very person who later went on to record a few of my songs and eventually, I did hear them played on the radio, and I realized how incredible his power is. I will not say that there haven't been obstacles in my life, but I will tell you that each obstacle that has been presented in my life I have been able to accept as part of my spiritual growth and while crossing into that valley while in this process, I have received amazing and glorious blessings. In recovery, I have had the opportunity to see daily progress in my life. I have known what it is to go from sleeping in the streets during bitter winters to eventually buying my own home. I have been able to share everything I have with my friends in friendship, kindness, and compassion, and I have met people who have given me what they have without expecting nothing in return. I remember so well their kindnesses to me when they didn't even know me; in 1991 when I got my first apartment, these loving people asked me one after another what I needed for my new place and each and every one of them came to my humble space with amazing goodness and they helped me to furnish my apartment so that I could live comfortably. Never in my life had I ever known people such as these, and for that, I feel incredibly grateful for having such friends with incredible kindness and compassion and I have known people who have offered me what they have with no expectations in return. It has been through these examples that my hardened rock of a heart began to soften and I have noticed how beautiful it is to help the less fortunate than yourself, and during the time that I have had in recovery, I try daily to offer of myself since the examples that I have received have made an impact within me which is different than the one I used to have. If after reading this work you may remember that part when I spoke of my sister who was born after me and where I explained how my Grandmother had given her up for adoption, and I never got to know her after my Mother was murdered by Don Julio. One day while I was in prayer with my God, I asked him to please put her into my life again and after many, many years of not knowing of her whereabouts, one day as I sat in my living room watching TV my telephone rang, and that phone call that I received transformed that prayer into yet another reality in my life. I feel greatly blessed to receive the blessings that my God has granted me and I know that he knew the emotional pain that I felt in my life and that spiritual desperation that tortured me for so many years. By him finding that lost link in my life which I had missed so greatly, that has been the greatest gift that my God has given me. There is nothing in the world like that family/blood connection, and that prior loss in my life was something so incredible to me. In 1999, I had the opportunity to finally meet my sister at Newark Airport, ad it was the most amazing experience that I have yet been able to experience in my life. That day when I saw her walk through those gates, I knew that she was my sister before I even got a good look at her. It was as if I was seeing and meeting my Mother's presence since the resemblance was uncanny and I could have never imaging that there would exist such a humble and gentle person within her being. I know very well that if had been Still lost in that darkness that I had found myself, this would have never happened and I would not have been able to experience the heights of incredible emotion in my heart since in the past, I lacked the ability to feel anything. In life we have the ability to accept certain things with confidence since we believe that we deserve them and we abuse those people that we have around us by taking advantage of what they offer us, and we're oblivious to this. In my past, I was that way and I use and abuse of the blessings that were offered to me by other people until they got tired of my ingratitude because such was constant. I will tell you a story so that you can see an example of what it is to feel grateful for the people who truly care about me today and what it really means to me. Since my childhood, I never had the good fortune of celebrating a birthday where my friends could share that day with me when the grace of God allowed me to see yet another day. On this day in the kitchen of my house, a few of my friends were gathered talking and my friend Mary reminded me that it was just a few days until my birthday and I told her that for me, that date was just like any other day in my life and that since I had never had the opportunity to ever have a birthday celebration, that was just not important for me. This is where I'm going to give you the example. My friend Mary and my friend Joe had made hundreds of sneaky plans behind my back to give me something that I had never enjoyed before, and they did it with all of their hearts and while I was still in the dark to what they were scheming, there were times when I felt angry with Mary due to some of the things that I would hear her talk on the phone with my other friends. While they planned my surprise birthday party, they resorted to many forms of deception to be able to carry out the plan. One day while I was with Mary sitting in front of her house, I overheard her talking on the phone with another man and this made me very uncomfortable so I excused myself and I told her that

I was going home. The other man that she was talking to happened to be my friend Joe since they were finalizing the details of my surprise birthday party and they were almost done with everything. Yet, I had gotten angry since my insecurities had created a mental block in my mind; Mary and Joe had pulled out all of my friends phone numbers from my cell phone behind my back, and they had "conspired" to have a surprise party for me. On that day, August 13th, I had the good fortune of getting for the first time something that I Had never had before for which my friends went through a lot of trouble to organize. When I later went by her house to pick her up, she invited me out for a drive and she and Joe had planned everything so well that I later felt uncomfortable with myself for having doubted her intentions towards me. When we got back to my house, the backyard was full of people – friends from New York, New Jersey, my daughter and many others, and it was then that I noticed what it is to leave a good impression in people's lives who surround you often. I know quite well that this love I had never experienced before in my life and I know that those blessings in my past I probably would have accepted with confidence, yet in these instance, I could see the genuine love of my friends take me to a place where today I find myself incredibly grateful with the blessings that God gives me daily. Maybe this event may not have too much importance for you, and maybe you have already had these blessings and you have accepted these with an attitude of entitlement thinking that perhaps that this is the obligation of others, but this is not the case. In other words, when I was lost, I would have taken something like that for granted thinking that people owed me this experience, and I probably would have even complained about the birthday presents since I never would have had the ability to be grateful for anything! It has taken me many years in recovery to correct this way of seeing things, and it has taken much work to notice these things in my life which in the past I would have never perceived since my mental maladjustments had me in complete darkness with regard to any blessings. Throughout this narrative I have given you some basic examples of my life while in constant physical, mental and spiritual breakdown, and I have given you numerous anecdotes of the degree of loss that existed in my personal life, and if you can identify through this story and not compare, it could be that clarity might reach your mind which is so appropriate to begin your spiritual journey once you're able to get out of that mental darkness in which you're used to living. All of the prior examples given have been in areas of my own mental loss and all of them are connected with the other to make your life into a garbage can of personal destruction, and it is only when you begin to see your growth manifest the glow that your dull spirit has lost with the destruction that you encountered throughout your personal trajectory. The fact that I have this disease of alcoholism doesn't grant me special benefits, nor am I gifted with some awesome knowledge, yet neither do I feel inferior to anyone nor better to anyone else; it only let's me know about what is happening within me. This disease is not a death sentence for me unless I decide to once again put that poison into my body, and only then will my physical, mental and spiritual destruction will begin again. I can honestly say that once all of these mental maladjustments are correctly examined, your spirit will find a freedom never beforehand experienced, and only then will you find the ability to be able to see life in another way. If you think that once your ego, your hate, your resentments, your insecurities, your grandiosity, your machismo, your jealousy, your low self-esteem, and your rage will be gone and that life is not going to present you with obstacles, then you're quite confused since life will continue giving you everything that you had before, but the difference is that you have begun to learn who you are and now you have another way of accepting what you can see according to your level of acceptance. It was my maladjusted emotions and my sick feelings that sent me on a journey of pure mental destruction and it has been under arduous work that today I find myself where I do today in a different place with my physical, mental, and spiritual recovery. This doesn't' mean that this makes me immune to this destructive disease since I don't want to feel at ease with myself and I forget about that dark hole that I had to the luck to get out of. I have had the opportunity of sharing my life in recovery with hundreds of people from different educational levels some of them doctors, lawyers, psychologists, firefighters, police officers – and various other people with much academic knowledge, and I have had the opportunity to witness how this disease of alcoholism doesn't discriminate against anyone, and it attacks both those in high class society as well as the middle and the poor class; it's a disease that destroys the lives of families and communities. My experience with this malady is that this disease will drag you to the deepest part of the abyss of darkness where dignity, respect, morals, and all productive values that make a human being useful in life are lost, and where death, jails, and psychiatric hospitals will be a part of your existence for the rest of your miserable life and the lives of other people a pure personal hell. I have witnessed on many occasions how many people have repaired their lives and then have become positive instruments in their community, and I have seen how so many people regain the respect of their families and acquire the ability to be productive once again in their lives, and I have also seen how a great number of people lose their lives for not surrendering in time before this terrible disease. I never want to see myself as someone who knows it all since I want to remain humble enough to learn something new every day. When I arrived at the doors of recovery on the 2nd of November of 1990, they explained to me that the only requirement to be a member is to have an honest desire to stop drinking, and it was that honest desire that helped me to get out of that dark world where I had wasted my existence. I stayed to repair the maladjusted way with which I used to think, and the blessings I have received have been incredible in the process of my journey. Once the obsession and compulsion for this poison disappeared from me, it was explained to me that now it was when the real work would begin, and this work would be for life and that it is only when I work with my character, that is when I will be able to see the fruits of that labor manifest and I will see the freedom that I will get. I will tell you that the freedom that my chained spirit to those destructive substances has experienced has been the most glorious thing that God has gifted me with since I'm no longer a slave to the mental deception to which I was enslaved in my past. Today, my past doesn't dictate my present, yet I do want to say that my past lets me know through those lived experiences where I was and where I find myself today, and I don't want to forget where I came from since if that were to happen, there might be the possibility that either prison, the psychiatric hospitals, or even death can again become my companions and in that same way, it can be that if I don't end up in those places, my life can become one of a painful existence where misery becomes my constant companion once again, and where my spirit cannot find peace in order to live full of the joy that I feel today in my heart. When I chose the title of this book "From Darkness to Light", I chose it with the purpose of letting the reader know that there are many areas in our lives which are in complete darkness and which we don't see for the simple reason that we have programmed ourselves with maladjusted behaviors throughout our growth which have been the cause of our spiritual decay. It has been under these learned behaviors that we have deteriorated mentally and we have perceived life with those mental maladjustments and I know very well that these mental maladjustments cause daily **derailments** to people and they can't accept them for the simple reason that they don't want to look at themselves. This story is not based on the mental maladjustments of the world in which I share my existence and neither did I put this words with the purpose of saving anyone from their own mental or spiritual agony. I only wrote it down with the hope that once examined, you can understand the degree of darkness that exists in our lives, and maybe through identification they can free themselves from their personal destruction with these destructive substances that have condemned all of us to. I know quite well that the use of these substances is a symptom of a greater maladjustment and I keep in mind that such substances were the cause of the appropriate escape so as not to perceive such maladjustments. I would like to tell the reader everything that I have learned in these years that I have spent in recovery. But it would be impossible to put all of that information in this writing since the two brain cells that I have left don't always work properly! It's a miracle that my God has granted me the ability to remember the greater part of my story after so many years in that mental destruction that I created for myself, and there are many other anecdotes of pure mental insanity which are not necessary to tell since they all go to the same place into the personal destruction of a human being. Yet I will tell you that if you have a desire of stopping the use of these poisons, I can honestly tell you that this can be achieved day by day if you're willing to allow other people to help you. The only thing that you need is the desire to stop, and once you have that desire, God will help you to put this into practice every day, and little by little, your mental growth will begin and mental clarity will arrive where there once existed darkness, and your spirit will begin to develop now that you don't put those poisons into your system. Today, I realize that I'm not perfect and that I will never be perfect, yet I know that it is my right every day to fight to try to be the best person that I can be. I remember very well that in my past I would lie to myself by telling myself that I didn't need anyone to help me and what I achieved with this lie was to create a personal entanglement in my life. Today I thank those very patient and tolerant and caring people who never rejected me yet who with pure love reconstructed my erratic life and my maladjusted way of thinking and today I feel extremely grateful that my wounded heart no longer feels that misery that I once felt. I have been able to feel unconditional love for those people like myself who suffer from such personal destruction. I will share that no one truly knows the deplorable level of emotional pain that leads a person to diminish to the point of physical **decline,** and I can honestly say that my descent was such that it was a miracle that God rescued me from such mental, physical, and spiritual destruction and it's in this way that my daily gratitude keeps me in peace with myself. I now that it doesn't matter the quantity of love that others had given me in my past and what they would have done to help me to get out of the mental obscurity in which I found myself, and I know that their efforts would have meant nothing to me since my level of rebellion and my self-pity towards myself and all of those other examples that I have outlined in this reading to be able to correct my destructive ways of looking at life. It was the lack of God in my life which didn't allow me to see all of my mental and spiritual maladjustments that I had. I would like to honestly say that my work with myself has ended and that I am now a "perfect" product that shines like a polished diamond. Yet, I don't want to lie to myself since I know that day by day, I have to remain vigilant about myself. I've had the opportunity to in my personal journey to acquire knowledge in various areas of my life which today I can dedicate the proper amount of time to gain a certain amount of personal satisfaction, and I find myself extremely grateful with the clarity that my God has granted me to be able to understand them. Throughout this journey, I have had the opportunity to understand that if a person do not repair his erratic way of thinking, and he doesn't attend to the skeletons that they have in their closet, there wouldn't exist a human being strong enough to "fix" such a person since the desire to change doesn't exist within him/her. I know that I have no power over the mental disturbances that other people around me create for themselves, and I know that my only right is to attend to myself since I can't "fix" any of their maladjustments. Yet in the process, the only thing that I know is that I can offer what It was offered for free to me, and if it works for them, I cannot be the one to take credit for such a thing; the credit belongs to God'. It is for this reason that I need to place my attention solely on myself. When I know what is unbalanced within me, when I understand that my disease is for life, when I stop lying to myself, when I stop looking for excuses in my life to run away daily from my situations is when I can live my life daily to the fullest. My acceptance today dictates the right way of living since I know that it's not the world around me with their maladjustments which makes up my personality. I know that every day I have to make changes in my personality to accommodate this world in which I wasted my existence. I know this because I try to live a decent life and this doesn't mean that other people around me want to live the way that I want. I know that I am responsible for the people that are removed from my life and when this happens, I need to see the reason behind it. I also know that there are hundreds of people that I don't want to waste time with since their behaviors affect my state of peace and create disturbances within me so its best to keep them away from me. Today I have the right to choose the people with whom I will spend my time and those people who don't produce anything positive for me are removed from my life since its best to be alone than to be in bad company. My God has granted me enough common sense to be able to look at myself daily and looking at my life with personal respect, and I don't associate with people who live their lives involve with those malevolent substances. In the same way, I don't blame anyone for having lived lost in their lives since I was once that person. I remember daily that I have a sick body and a mind that I can not trust since it deceived me for so many years. My mental agony and emotional pain that I carried locked within myself was what took me into my own spiritual loss, and today, I am immensely grateful to be able to understand my life with more mental clarity. I know only too well that the same way that I suffered there are thousands of people suffering daily and it's sad to see the degree of destruction that they do to themselves and to others since they can't see their own mental insanity in which they find themselves since what exists is darkness in their lives. I know it's necessary for me to keep in contact with these people who suffer from this disease and who every day teach me how you can live without these poisons. It's very important to have a place where I need to go to find the answers that I need to keep myself away from these destructive substances and to be able to correct my disoriented way of seeing life, and it's in this place that we frequently find the appropriate peace to understand this malady. In the past, I never had anyone that I could trust or that I could call a friend since I thought that once you knew what I was, you would reject me and would judge me due to my maladjustments. Yet it was later explained to me that I would have to learn to trust something and that was very difficult for me since my insecurities never allowed such a thing. In recovery I have a sponsor who is more than a friend – he's my eyesight, and my mind when mine isn't working properly, and he is more than family for me since I never had a person in which I could put all of my trust in completely. I have a large family and the good thing about that is that it doesn't matter in what part of the world I find myself they also find themselves there too, there is, always someone to help me. In my past, I had associates whose interests were based on the quantity of monetary benefits that we could get while we got the poisons that we wanted, and once that happened, there were many times when we tried to kill each other. Never in the years that I was incarcerated did any of these acquaintances came to visit me or wrote me to send me a warm greeting. Yet in the time that I have spent living my life in recovery, I have people who are daily in my life who I can truly consider to be true friends. Today I don't project about the things that I want to get since I don't want to disillusion myself with such projections since I know that by doing so is like counting your chickens before they hatch. Every day I try not to make plans since I know that most of the time, they don't turn out like I plan them and I have adapted to living day by day since the final result is easier to accept. What I wish to share is not done with the purpose of putting negative ideas into your minds about mental and spiritual recovery. Once you understand your problem and you decide that you don't want to live the way you used to and if you were to arrive at the doors of recovery, you have to realize that you're going to be under the company of other people like yourself who have suffered from numerous inconsistencies in their lives, and you must remember that not everyone recovers at the same rate and that you're going to find many people in these places who perhaps don't practice what they learn. You might be able to see many areas of inconsistencies within them, and then you will understand just how disastrous is that darkness in which such people live. Just because people have stopped drinking for a certain period of time this doesn't mean that they are working with themselves to become decent people and you will learn in time that a leopard will always be tagged as a leopard by its spots. Then it will be within you to select those people in your recovery who can bring something constructive into your life if that's what you want. There are various descending steps which lead the alcoholic to descend down to the precipice of personal desolation, and not all of the alcoholics that I have had the opportunity of knowing have descended to the same depths that others have descended to, but I will tell you that it doesn't matter to what depths you sink to if you can get out, that is a miracle. I know quite well that the losses that I have had have been of great proportions especially when it concerns my family, and I know that I am never going to recover what was lost. Yet I know that today what I have received has no price. This disease daily has one human being in this world in complete darkness and I know well that that human being could be me. There are many people who are waiting for liver transplants, and I have known people that the damage that this disease has caused them has left them with a brain in a state of decomposition so disastrous that they don't even know what is happening in their surroundings since they have become pure human vegetables, and I know that this can always be me. It is for that reason that I give thanks to my God for these blessings since I wasn't supposed to still be here alive offering you these stories of mental insanity and to where my alcoholism took me. At these same moments while I'm writing this story of mental insanity created by the consumption of alcohol, in hundreds of homes the destruction of these substances have someone's wife or lover living under pure terror since some member of their family is terrorizing them under the influence of alcohol. In hundreds of homes, there are children paying the consequences of the destruction that a member of their family is bringing to their home and where perhaps there will be another little boy or another little girl carrying the scars of family violence brought about when these poisons are taken by one of their parents, either their mother, their father or any other family member. There are hundreds of people who after one night of partying will end up in a hospital emergency room since under an alcoholic psychosis, they tried to take their lives. There will also be cases in which hundreds of people under the influence of this poison find themselves locked up in prison since under a blackout the took someone else's life and they didn't realize what destruction they created. I also know that hundreds of people at the steering wheel have caused the death of others people and liquor has been part of that misery. While I relate these terrible realities, I will also share that there is recovery, but you have to be sick and tired of being sick and tired, and when you decide that you had enough misery, and you've had enough mental and spiritual desolation, maybe then you will get the clarity that will grant you the freedom from your self-created hell. It was my sick feelings and my sick mental maladjustments which took me to the edge of the darkness where the emotional pain and desperation made my life a monster to live with, and it was those substances which destroyed me daily and that kept me hostage in a disgusting mental prison. The agonies that I suffered cannot be perceived by the mind of any human being since no one had the fortune of walking in my shoes to the deepest and darkest spot of the hell where God saw fit to rescue me from. If today you were to find me in a restaurant or a store and you would set your eyes on me, you wouldn't be able to see a sign on my forehead which would read, "I am an alcoholic." I am a human being like everyone else who every day keeps in mind where he was then and where he is today, and I don't want to forget where I came from and what was it that took me to that state of spiritual decay. I'm not someone who deserves any special treatment just because I have this disease. I am only one of millions who day by day attend to their mental state without putting any garbage into their system in order to destroy my spirit which has blossomed like never before. In this writing I have given you very important facts for the mental growth of a person and areas of sick growth within a human being, and I have not achieved this just because I have long titles of psychology or a doctorate in medical science. I have only achieved these things because for many years, I have been able to realize where the majority of these examples presented here have infected my life and have caused numerous detours in my life; they are all each connected one with the other within a human being and it makes a person who doesn't recognize the degree of darkness in which they live daily. They are the ones that cause the sick, maladjusted feelings and deplorable behaviors in a human being, and they make alcohol and the use of other substances attractive to you. It might be that some of the people whom might read this work may get some negative ideas about the life that I lived and it might be that other people may come to understand the degree of emotional pain and all of the sick feelings which took me to such a destructive prison, and I will tell you that neither the suffering and the pain that I have witnessed nor the physical, verbal or sexual abuse have been greater than that destruction which I create within myself. There does not exist a punishment or a prison or a mental asylum more painful than the prison that a human being creates in their own mind, and there are no medications for psychiatric treatment which can control the destruction that is created in such a place. It was in this desolate place within my being that the escapes from life began and where I created destructive ideas to be able to run away from my pain, and that race was made easy while searching for an easy death. Yet one day, when I got to the end of my rope, the only thing that it took was a heartfelt plea from the deepest part of my soul direct to my God so that the doors of hell would open and I could once again return back to the reality which today isn't so hard to swallow. PSYCHIATRIC TREATMENT – in all the years that I sought psychiatric help, there was always a place in my mind which was only mine and I gave to the doctors everything else but that space in order to remain sick mentally and spiritually. It was while hanging on to those secrets that I made other peoples lives a personal disaster. I don't wish the harm that I created for myself on anyone else in this world since today I know that no one deserves such pain, and it's a shame that every day, I see how other human beings are lost in that darkness where they want to keep seeing themselves as victims and not like survivors. What I'm going to tell you next is not done with the goal of making the psychiatric profession seem like morons or people without knowledge of the tasks that they take on to help those people who suffer from grave mental problems. Yet the experiences that I have lived in my past which have taught me about the mistakes that such people make, and the incorrect diagnoses that they render upon so many patients. I know that I must thank such doctors for having used me like a guinea pig to try out all of those medications that for so many years of my life I saw myself forced to take, and in the same way that I thank them, it's the same way that I feel a certain degree of indignation against them for having kept me as a "zombie" for all of the years that they kept me under their scrupulous treatment. It's amazing that with all of the advanced progress of today that science is still so blind about human beings, and during all of the psychiatric hospitalizations that I endured and all of those years that I spent drugged up they could never detect that my bipolar illness could have been diagnosed with a simple blood test which would have let them know that my condition only required that they give me medication to control my thyroid gland which was out of balance during all of the years that I found myself in that depressive state where I constantly searched for death to find me. Although these doctors had their advanced titles and degrees in terms of mental health was concerned they seemed to need those medications more than I did, maybe through their inconsistent efforts at least they prevented me from committing suicide (although their methods left me with a bad taste for the profession.) Today I thank Dr. Scott M. for having been responsible for returning me to a mental state that I have never before experienced in all of the years that I sought medical treatment. Thanks to Dr. Scott M. all of those previous medications have been substituted by a simple pill called Sintroid, and my depressive state and suicidal urges have disappeared. Throughout all of the years that I sought psychiatric help, I have never before felt the freedom that I feel today, and my spirit that was chained to all of those psych meds, alcohol, and controlled substances never allowed me the freedom that I feel today. I realize that I had to go through everything that I went through to get to where I am today, and it has been all of my life experiences which have taught me throughout my life that there exists a God who is merciful and compassionate and loving towards those who suffered like I did. In the process of sharing with you the life that I have lived and through all of the lost pathways in which I found myself, it's very important to tell you that my life today is like a paradise compared with that desolate and dark hell that I lived in, and I can't take credit for such a blessing since that credit belongs to that God that I didn't know and who was that one that I blamed for all of the misery and pain that I had in my existence. Today I work daily with the way that I perceive life since I was the one who made that life a dumpster of pain and my mental recovery is something that I work with every day since I know that my soul is finally free from the destruction that I caused to it. Only I can entrap my spirit again in that former misery if I didn't tend to my inside and it's working from within that I gain that daily freedom to live a life full of gratitude. If I told you that I am perfect, I would be full of grandiosity if I said that I never feel angry sometimes I would be lying, yet it's the way that I resolve my anger that I will then resolve those situations that are presented to me which let me know that there is a certain degree of progress in my life since my God has granted me the ability to examine myself daily in order to see the progress within. I feel compassion today for those who are lost in that mental darkness just like I was, and I know just how deep that darkness is since I lived in it daily for so many, many years. Today, I try to offer a kind and soothing word to that neighbor that I hated for so many years. Today, I feel unconditional love for this world that I perceive every day and I try my best to be decent with everyone else who is suffering. It's also important to have a mind that's positive and constructive since I know where negativity took me and when it rears it's ugly head, I can see it and reject it since today, I know who I am. I don't feel that destructive desperation that I used to feel, and my spirit no longer suffers from that incredible desolation that I felt in the past. When I gave my heart to God, he granted me the necessary freedom to be able to feel love that had never before existed within my heart. There is not doubt in my heart today what our God has done with my pained soul, and I can daily see where I am on the path since He freed me from the destruction that I afforded my spirit for so many years, and that heavy baggage that I carried in my insides has disappeared little by little. Please don't misunderstand this message and keep an open mind and if in this story you find something that might be helpful to you, please accept it as a gift from God since the glory is His, not mine. Keep in mind that suffering is unnecessary when there is faith, and its that which transports us through the abysses that we must go through. This story is not based in a **12-Step program**, and although God brought me to this place where I find myself today, and I am now here. Although I have used numerous examples about recovery and what the concepts of the 12-Step program has gifted me, this story is, after all, based on my personal life and all of the areas of darkness that exist trapped inside of the human brain which transform certain people into constant ogres within humanity. This story is not written with the purpose of telling the reader where he/she must go to get help for their maladjusted way of looking and reacting at life. It has been written with the purpose and the hope that if examined and similarities are found and you can keep an open mind in your life maybe you can take the right decision so that you can once again find the clarity that your suffering soul so richly deserves. If you had the good fortune of finding the purpose that God has for you and your loved ones, that would be a blessing. Today, I know that God used many people in my surroundings to give relief to my spirit that so needed it, and it's my belief that daily, He does this in my life through the examples that other people give me. This means that if you need a psychiatrist to help you, this is not bad since your seeking improvement for yourself. If you need a 12-Step program, that's good since your looking to better yourself, yet if knowing that you have a problem with these destructive substances and you do nothing to make it better, then you will suffer a life of mental and spiritual desolation where darkness will be your constant prison and where you will rip apart the life from those people who love and appreciate you. There has to come a moment in your life where the only thing that separates you from those damned substances is God who can heal you from your personal agony. I wish to say that if God rescued me when I was a twisted tree, He can rescue anyone from their personal destruction. I only pray that those that are suffering as I did may once again find the ability to find that freedom from this disease so that they can once more become useful people within society. A person cannot recover on their own willpower from the darkness that exists in the deepest part of their fragmented mind unless they surrender before the concept that it is God who controls your life, and it's only when you can accept this fact that you will find the liberation from the agony you've suffered. I've had the opportunity of witnessing how numerous people relapse back into this terrible disease since they find themselves content and complacent with their lives and they lose the ability to look at this disease with respect, and they have fooled themselves again just like in their past. In order for someone who has been submerged in that dark lagoon of alcoholism and addiction to find freedom from that horrible state, they must accept that only a Higher Power can save them, and once that Higher Power is accepted into their heart, only then will that freedom of their soul lost in that mire of personal destruction find its desired liberation. Yet if you arrive at the doors of recovery and there is no faith in your heart, don't think that there's something wrong with you, and if all you have is blind faith and you have the desire to stop taking those poisons, there will come a day in your recovery when clarity will begin to appear in your mind and slowly but surely you will begin to find your way since you'll no longer find yourself so lost as you once were. Believe me when I tell you that in my life, there never existed Faith, and it took me a few years in recovery so that my mind could accept and so that my heart would surrender to this concept, and I will say that it has been the miracles that I have been able to witness in my life which today let me know how incredible the power of our God is. Today, I know that I was a leper inside, and my God has removed that leprosy from inside of my mind and my heart, and I find myself very grateful for that blessing. There are many avenues of escape for the person who is infected with this disease of alcoholism and addition to controlled substances, and they all very sickeningly condition themselves inside of a maladjusted mind of a person; it's those escapes that are not seen by the person which take them to a **precipice/edge of** mental darkness where there is no light so that they can see the devastation to their wounded spirit which continues to pay the consequences of such destruction daily, and it is only when you are able to see such maladjustments that you will be able to find that freedom which you have created. What I have accomplished with this reading is to list the facts of all of those maladjustments form which people suffer and the **pathways/avenues** of recovery for them, and I will tell you that once they are witnessed within your structural makeup, if clarity begins to surge within you, you will then surrender to the truth of the seriousness of your condition and you will begin the task of spiritual reconstruction. You will also notice how your perception of humanity will change, and your behaviors will also change little by little. In this book I have outlined numerous facts about my personal life and my physical mental, and spiritual demise, and I will say that although many people have perhaps experienced the emotional agony that I have experienced due to the murder of my Mother, maybe still some of you may not fully understand since they didn't experience this as I did. Yet, I know that while I used as copouts the deaths of my parents, the sexual and physical abuse I suffered, none of those situations took me to that state of spiritual decay with such speed as alcohol and controlled substances did. It is with this mental clarity that I have managed to transform a life of pain and mental agonies and maladjustments into something positive and constructive to give it to whomever can use it to get something good out of it. No prison, no mental asylum, no loss of material possessions or money caused the impact in my life that those poisons caused me and I will confess that once I saw the problem and dealt with accordingly, my life chained to that destructive prison found the freedom to live with a free spirit. Yet I will tell you that if I had not dealt with all of those mental maladjustments which I have previously mentioned, there may have been a possibility that I would still find myself emotionally sick. I pray to God that this story is helpful to ANYONE who is suffering physically, mentally or spiritually and that it may be helpful to bring some mental clarity to the place where there was only darkness in your spirit. It was alcohol and controlled substances which took me to the demise that I had the fortune to experience, and it was only then when I could accept such a thing that my live took another turn.

God,
Grant me the Serenity
To
Accept the Things
I Cannot Change
The
Courage to Change
The
Things that I Can
And
The Wisdom to Know the Difference

www.ingramcontent.com/pod-product-compliance
Lightning Source LLC
Chambersburg PA
CBHW020302290526
45784CB00003B/1327